THE LAWYER
WHO ROCKED
THE UNITED NATIONS

Biography of
Vaikuntha Vasan

Satha Ananthan

Red Fort Publications
London

THE LAWYER WHO ROCKED
THE UNITED NATIONS ©

First Edition, March 2003

Printed and Published by
Red Fort Publications
55, Warren Road, Colliers Wood
London SW19 2HY, UK
Tel: 020-8542 9787
e-mail: gandeevasan@hotmail.com

Contents

Prologue

History is decorated in fullness with great personalities who influenced change or transformed the destiny of societies. This work is about such a hero, his achievements and his life. A hero who's relentless campaign influenced change in remarkable but subtle ways. A change affecting the destiny of the Tamil Nation in the Island of Sri Lanka. The larger than life lawyer-who's extraordinary actions merit attentive analysis by all students and researchers in the socio-political faculties. This is a modern biography in conception. Concise and pointed to be a reference book.

I was pleasantly taken aback when Krishna Vaikuntha Vasan telephoned and summoned me, to become his Biographer. I had only just recovered from the arduous publishing and promotion efforts of my book on economics. Hesitating but yearning to grasp the deal, I said: why not? And the first meeting was fixed in his south London home. As the editor of London Murasu Tamil magazine of the 70s and 80s, I was made to understand that I was more qualified to write a book on him than anyone else. It was only during that time Vaikuntha Vasan had reached his peak of achievements, of which I was a keen witness. The biography was authorised to be produced.

Vaikuntha Vasan was not an ordinary lawyer. Nor was he a campaigner like many we know. A Socialist at heart he was the Secretary-General of the public service trade union – the Government Clerical Service Union (GCSU) of Ceylon. A pioneering and campaigning journalist of the 50s, he boldly challenged the conservative right wing government of Ceylon during that time. Having been an active trade unionist, he had trav-

-lled around the world penning his travel writing books. While all this was happening, he qualified as a Barrister, practised for a decade as a successful advocate of the Supreme Court; and in 1971 took up post as District Judge in Zambia. He brushed shoulders with the African leaders. And turned a political campaigner hot on the heels of arriving in London in the late 70s. Vaikuntha Vasan became a household name in the Tamil diaspora, with his uninvited ascent onto the speaker's rostrum in the United Nations on 5th of October 1978. He did not stop there...

The shelves of the book world is filled with biographies and autobiographies of all types of personalities: Royalty, Politicians, Showbiz, Super rich, Business magnates, Sportspersons, Terrorists et al. Even the most abused have produced their biographies. The burgeoning biography industry has lost its bearing; money and more money is the only focus. This biography is not without a bearing. It is full of salient features and lessons. Weaving through the history of the struggles of the enterprising Tamil Nation of Sri Lanka. Of how one man walking alone like a lion, peacefully and strategically attained a few remarkable feats- big and small. How an individual with lesser power and finance had engineered change, without being much noticed.

Vaikuntha Vasan, is a world phenomena whose messages and acts will go down in history to be treasured for a long time to come. He rocked the United Nations with his transcendental message: ***Minorities abound this earth; and they have a right to voice their grievances!*** His proclamation in front of the ambassadors from 150 nations also meant that this world body could no longer be a place for pomp and pageantry; a mouthpiece for a few powers, and to survive as a rubber stamp organisation. Events ever since the United Nations was created had only proved Vaikuntha Vasan had a case. And it is growing more and more to be so...

People's Voice – the only independent English Newsweekly edited and published from Colombo by Vaikuntha Vasan in the 1950s was a masterpiece of bold reporting that championed the cause of the masses of the Island nation. In each and every editorial he lashed out intelligently at the oppressive and devious mechanisms adopted by the right wing government. The cartoons were witty. An island in abundance of natural resources and intellectual powers steeped in poverty? The entire gamut of socio-politico-economic fields were under scrutiny. They hold as models even in today's context of extreme capitalism suffered by most nations. Vaikuntha Vasan upheld the motto: *Victory to the People* through his People's Voice. Providentially the archives of the newspapers are still available in bound form for the benefit of future generations.

Vaikuntha Vasan created a base in London to co-ordinate his campaigns: He became the convenor of the Tamil Co-ordinating Committee. From this base he went about uniting the various factions operating in the Tamil struggle all over the world. He met the Indian Prime Minister Indira Gandhi, presented a memo to the Pope, and attended seminars and meetings worldwide. Vaikuntha Vasan's successful intervention against the deportation order of a Tamil girl in Norway in 1979, also lead on his discovery and establishing of "Norway as an important country that is very sympathetic to the cause of Sri Lankan Tamils". Links were strengthened with Norway from then on.

His vision more than two decades ago for an Indo-Ceylon Federation based on the European Common Market model, leading to a South Asian Federation was a truly outstanding brainwork. The subsequent formation of the South Asian Area Regional Co-operation(SAARC) and the growing economic affinity between India and Sri Lanka proves how Vaikuntha Vasan was astute in his thoughts. Due credit goes to him for persisting that the regional super power India had a major role to play - if the Sri Lankan crisis is to be solved. Year 2002 is witnessing this prophesy of Vaikuntha Vasan; as also the role Norway is playing.

The Lawyer who rocked the United Nations is not a biography in the traditional grove. Biographies are flooding the market at an astronomical scale. Publishing consumerism is now aiming for mass appeal of scandals, pop culture, cinema, football, crime, terrorism and anything that satisfies the basic instincts. They are copious to the hilt with minor details. Getting out of the stereotype frame, this book intends to create a new age type biography. Serving as a reference book for the intellectually oriented and socially conscious. Compact with information that will be useful and also lessons to be learned.

A massive political and media power exists to promote only their chosen personalities in every facet of life. Exploring and restoring unsung heroes and suppressed talents in the fields of science, technology, arts, culture, religion, social service, business and politics - is also an objective that is a pressing need.

As small hinges opening big doors-the lawyer rocking into the United Nations has opened the insights into the vast spread and role this Institution plays in global affairs. His travelogue brings out the high quality of humane life prevalent in two socialist countries. Finally, presenting the concise history of the Pearl of the Indian Ocean-Sri Lanka. I invite the readers now to move on and join up with Vaikuntha Vasan onto his Life Story...

Chapter 1

United Nations Rocked

The heights by great men reached and kept
were not attained by sudden flight,
But they, while their companions slept,
were toiling upward in the night.   *-Longfellow*

The United Nations General Assembly was in full session on 5th of October 1978; lunch recess was to come soon. The President of Cyprus has already delivered his hour-long speech, followed by the Prime Minister of Surinam.The President of the Assembly   Indalecio Liveano invited the Sri Lankan Foreign Minister to speak next. Upto 2000 delegates were in the Assembly when the next speaker came to the rostrum. Returning the greeting by the President, with the ritual bow, he addressed:

Mr. President! Leaders of the World!
If oppressed minority nations such as Tamil Eelam cannot make representations to this supreme body, then where are we to go?

My name is Krishna and I come from the 2 ½ million strong Nation of Tamil Eelam lying between Sri Lanka and India.

The Sri Lanka Sinhala government is continuing a policy of genocide aimed at the destruction of our Tamil Nation.

We have exercised our right of self-determination to live as a separate Nation.

There is every danger of the Tamil problem threatening the peace of the Indian Region.

The problem in Sri Lanka will develop to be as serious as the Palestinian and the Cyprus problems unless you, the world leaders intervene and help in its solution now.

We appeal to you for such help! Thank you. I apologise for speaking without permission.
LONG LIVE TAMIL EELAM!

The speaker was unquestionably not the foreign minister of Sri Lanka, Shaul Hameed, who was still seated in his chair spell-bound. Krishna Vaikuntha Vasan had successfully carried out his daring act in the presence of delegates from 150 nations gathered in this world political assembly. Not many understood at that time, the historical impact of this bold accomplishment. To hold sway of the podium of the top apex world body for two minutes, Vaikuntha Vasan should have plucked up tremendous courage. A courage mounteth with conviction and the occasion.

The BBC World News was the first of the media to break the news:

"At the U.N. General Assembly there has been a demonstration in support of Tamil minority in Sri Lanka. Just as the foreign minister was approaching the rostrum to speak, a man rushed forward and said he wanted to make an appeal on behalf of the Tamils, who he said were victims of genocide by the Sri Lankan government." The BBC news added that "the microphone was cut off and the man was led away by a guard. The protester was later identified as a former Sri Lankan judge now living in London."

The BBC Correspondent further added:

"Mr. K. Vaikuntha Vasan announced himself at the rostrum as Mr. Krishna. He said he wanted to speak on behalf of the 3.5million Tamils, who he said were the victims of genocide by what he called the Sinhala government. At this point he was taken out of the building by guards. Later he managed to get back inside one of the public areas where he was interviewed by one of the BBC Correspondents."

"He had been a judge for several years in East Africa and now a lawyer in London. He had been at a legal Conference in America and decided to stay on to publicise the cause. He wanted to do something dramatic to draw the attention of the world to the plight of the Tamils, as other efforts have failed. He got in by mingling with a group of delegates there by avoiding the usual stringent security checks."

Vaikuntha Vasan's this dramatic act certainly drew the attention of the world press, radio and television to the plight of the Tamils of Sri Lanka.

Even the United Nations General Assembly's Provisional Verbatim Record of that twenty-second meeting of the Thirty-third session had listed under General debate: "Speech by Krishna (Tamil Eelam)"

Mr. Hameed the Foreign Minister of Sri Lanka was recorded to have said: "I wish to thank the previous speaker who tried to steal my opportunity and thereby create a little sensation".

It was the second unusual incident to have taken place in the rostrum of the General Assembly; On September 26th during the same session the Soviet Republic's Foreign Minister Andrei Gromyko keeled over at the rostrum while addressing and was assisted out of the hall by aides. He returned to complete his speech after an hour's rest; and complained that the lights in the Assembly hall was very bright and hot.

But in the 32 years of UN existence upto this incident; and in fact upto 2002, since its first meeting in January 1946; no radical organizations like the PLO, IRA, Red Guards or even the Baader-Meinhoff had ever attempted such a daring means of focussing world attention; as that was undertaken by Vaikuntha Vasan.

Debt of Gratitude

One of the first to acknowledge Vaikuntha Vasan with a debt of gratitude came from Mr.Amirthalingam, the leader of the Tamil United Liberation Front (TULF), the political party representing the Sri Lankan Tamils: "Mr. Vaikuntha Vasan has very succinctly brought out the case for self-determination of the Eelam Tamil Nation, and the need for Tamil national liberation from the Sinhala neo-colonialists."

He further said: "The pressing need of the hour is publicity among the nations of the world for the Tamil cause. Mr. Vaikuntha Vasan placed Tamil Eelam on the map of the world when he took the podium of the UN General Assembly before the Foreign Minister of Sri Lanka. The Tamil Nation owes a debt of gratitude to Mr. Vaikuntha Vasan for that master stroke."

The Tamil leadership had long felt the seemingly insurmountable political and publicity logistics that were involved in their struggle. The UN action had vanquished that hopeless situation. "Vaikuntha Vasan", said a political commentator, "has achieved much more for the Tamil cause by way of international publicity in his two minute raid on the UN microphone than the TULF has done so far". And so the path was paved for the internationalisation of the Tamil struggle.

Security lapse?

The natural reaction to what happened on October 5th resulted in the tightening of security measures at the UN Headquarters. Additionally to the beefing up of the security force; credentials of all delegates were closely examined from then on. But how did Vaikuntha Vasan manage to get inside the premises; let alone to the podium?

In its news report following the UN incident, the Independent Newspaper from Colombo raised the issue of an accomplice from within the United Nations who could have aided Vaikuntha Vasan. Ever since the speculation of an accomplice, till now, the mystery had remained unresolved. The Independent Newspaper quoted from the mouth of a former Sri Lankan UN Ambassador, Sir Senerath Gunawardene: "I know the workings of the UN office very well because of my close association with the UN. I am almost positive Vaikuntha Vasan could not have got into the delegates' seats without any help." Sir Senerath was not only Ambassador for Sri Lanka (1955-58) but also helmed the Human Rights Commission at the UN.

The Independent Newspaper went at length to prove the accomplice theory. UN attendence averages nearly 750 delegates at each session. This is worked out on the basis of five delegates to each of the 150 member nations. So that Vaikuntha Vasan who was earlier a judge in Zambia, representing that country at two Commonwealth Magistrates Conferences in Nairobi in August 1973 and again in Kuala Lumpur in August 1975; had contacts in all the African countries as well outside. Speculation points to the accomplice being from the Afro-Arab bloc which along with Asia dominates the UN. Vaikuntha Vasan was also a Marxist, the Independent quoted. Was there a security lapse then?

Modus Operandi

Vaikuntha Vasan had planned the whole operation in typical bank robber style from the moment he set foot in New York. Following the completion of his attending the Annual American Bar Association Conference, he had first met with C.V. Narasimhan, former Under-Secretary General of the United Nations. He wanted to find out from the Under-Secretary General, a fellow Tamilian from India, whether he could arrange for a speech to the General Assembly, by Mr Amirthalingam, the Sri Lankan Tamil leader, then visiting the US at the invitation of the State Department. 'If Palestinian Yasser Arafat could address the world assembly with no official authority why not Amirthalingam also do the same'? C.V. Narasimhan was not supportive; Arafat had the whole Arab world backing him; but what support had Amirthalingam?

Vaikuntha Vasan, a rebel even at the age of 58, had his own ingenious scheme. He started spending all of September visiting the UN like accredited delegates do. The only route for non-delegates was to take to the visitors' gate and then join a guided tour of the skyscraper on the East River. But Vaikuntha Vasan just walked in with his brief case through the delegates' entrance. He hurried past the security with a look of a harried delegate late for a crucial meeting. He would raise his left arm up to take a look at his wristwatch as though he was late.

With delegates of all nationalities, colours, costumes and accents, the security was not over-meticulous about identifications. Vaikuntha Vasan was fortunate at that. He was never stopped; although he had to muster cast iron determination and steel nerves to get in each time. And he became a familiar face to the security at the gates and inside. He wandered always looking busy. He mingled with delegates from all countries; in the canteen, as well as in diplomatic parties. And he had also met the Secretary General Kurt Waldheim at a party. If anybody asked him, he will in all honesty say that he is from Sri Lanka. And if he was asked which committee he was serving, as each belonged to some committee; he would say "well I haven't decided yet whether to accept the second committee or the third". For Vaikuntha Vasan all delegates he had aquainted throughout were his accomplices; of course they were all not aware of what he was planning to do. Here the accomplices theory falls apart.

Vaikuntha Vasan even took his seat in the delegates' section of the Assembly session. He suggested to himself that he was a delegate from Tamil Eelam – the Tamil state in Sri Lanka. He had no qualms about his plans. He believed that he represented his Tamil people and that if he is not given the opportunity to present their case, he would present it anyway. And on October 5th he flitted from delegation to delegation, chatting briefly, with his sharp focus on the Assembly President's call. And when the call came he just walked majestically to the rostrum.

Chapter 2

Strike while the iron is hot

Fame is the perfume of heroic deeds
                                              -Socrates

Vaikuntha Vasan's dramatic appearance at the United Nations on 5th October 1978 was a heroic deed which not only brought him fame; but a few remarkable outcomes. It was a symbolic but hair-raising act that had boosted the Tamil freedom movement. The blaze of global publicity that followed embarrassed the Sri Lankan government. There were political dimensions as well as international ramifications that unfolded.

A Shot in the Arm

The Sri Lankan Tamil freedom movement received a shot in the arm as a direct consequence of Vaikuntha Vasan raising his voice in the United Nations. This was also a primary outcome that spinned off other issues. The pre-eminent effect was the jolt delivered to the indecisive and powerless political leadership of the Tamil people.

The Tamil United Liberation Front (TULF) formed following the merger of the Tamil parties in May 1972; officially passed what was named the Vaddukoddai resolution in 1976, declaring Tamil Eelam aspiration as its mandate. While the Tamil Eelam militancy had already emerged in 1972 by way of student agitations and later on manifesting as the vanguard movement of Tamil Tigers; the political lethargy and opportunism of the TULF post-1976 was treading a path of hopeless route with no sense of direction. The demise in April 1977, of the undisputed leader of the Tamil people, S.J.V. Chelvanayagam – who was also the architect of the Tamil State, had left a vacuum. With a younger leader A.Amirthalingam at the helm, the TULF lacked imagination and it was failing to follow through its declared goal of Tamil Eelam. It was at this juncture the timely and imaginative action of Vaikuntha Vasan descended - to arouse the spirits of the Tamil party and the militants. He became a hero in the minds of men, women and youth and thereby perfuming into fame. But the most important stimulus that arose out of this shot in the arm went to the militant movement of Tamil New Tigers (TNT), which spread its wings and went into action with fervour. The flight of the eagle had by now begun.

The Agony of Sri Lanka

Proudly christened the pearl of the Indian ocean – Ceylon, and later Sri Lanka - had a high standing in global terms. As a tea garden of the world and with beautiful landscapes, there was a soft corner in the minds of all who knew the Island. The festering of communal riots plunging it into a state of turbulence was concealed to the outside world, despite the actions already online in India and in the UK by Tamil groups. Vaikuntha Vasan was the first to expose the vulnerability of the Island State to the international comity of nations.

The Sri Lankan government was in the midst of developing the Free Trade Zone(FTZ), the king-pin for the Island's economic progress; combined with aid procurement programmes from the World Bank and the donor countries. The embarrassment caused brought jitters to the government. There was grim and anger; with no means of extraditing the perpetrator of this action. For he had not violated any known law. And there was also a risk of amplifying the current exposure of bad publicity. But what Vaikuntha Vasan pioneered, from a historical perspective, was setting the stage free for an ever ready blaze of adverse publicity; each time the crisis in Sri Lanka worsened.

In the book "The Agony of Sri Lanka"(1983) written by former diplomat and senior foreign affairs official T.D.S.A. Dissanayake, the agony of the Sri Lankan government is portrayed thus: " …every now and then Eelam lobbyists abroad staged a publicity stunt geared to attract the attention of the media. Perhaps the most successful of them was the gimmick of Mr. Krishna Vaikuntha Vasan, a London based lawyer and Eelam supporter. In October 1978 he impersonated Foreign Minister A.C.S.Hameed to address the UN General assembly for a few minutes…However from the point of view of the media it was a sensational story at the expense of Sri Lanka."

The Sri Lankan governments had time and again suffered not merely from adverse publicity but from severe economic loss – through the loss of aid, investments and tourism revenues. This form of economic embargo and penalties could be construed as one of the causes that the Sri Lankan government had to eventually come to terms with the Tamil aspirations.

Consequential International Dimensions

There are very few men who are able to think and feel beyond the present moment. Vaikuntha Vasan is one of them. The brilliance of continuity engineered by this mastermind in creating international dimensions as a follow-up of his UN action is one such illustration. He strikes while the iron is hot.

David Astor-described as the greatest British Editor of the post-war era is no stranger for Vaikuntha Vasan. He had been in touch with this representative of the British aristocracy even prior to the UN affair. This time he was in touch with David Astor to report about his speech at the UN. While regretting that the British press failed to report the speech delivered at the UN, David Astor replied:

...I am, however, sending a copy of your speech to the Royal Institute of International Affairs (Chatham House) where I hope that it will be made available to students of such affairs as this. As you probably know, Chatham House is much frequented by journalists and government officials and is no means just an academic institution...

David Astor was righteously forthcoming when he pinpointed the importance of the Royal Institute of International Affairs (RIIA). Founded in 1920 and given the Royal Charter in 1926, with the monarch as its official head, the Royal Institute of International Affairs is situated at 10, St. James's Square in London. Otherwise called the "Chatham House", this is a highly powerful and secretive organisation wielding international influence and power of a higher degree. It is supported by global oil, banking and media corporations, including the BBC; and is closely linked to the Universities of Oxford and Cambridge; and the London School of Economics and Political Science.

The Royal Institute of International Affairs along with the Trilateral Commission, Council on Foreign Relations(CFR),

The Bilderberg Group, Club of Rome, and the United Nations, form part of the most powerful Round Table network in the world today. The Round Table, an elite secret group was found-ed in the last quarter of 19th century by Cecil Rhodes, the South African overlord. Rothschilds, Rockefellors, Windsors, Warburgs and Mellons-world's most powerful dynasties are among the prominent members of these Organisations. World's top bureaucrats Henry Kissinger and Lord Carrington are also members of these groups. In addition, the most influential per-sonalities from the academic, scientific, banking, business, political, media, medicine, military and intelligence sectors are initiated into, and meet regularly in the above Institutions, including the Royal Institute of International Affairs.

The Council on Foreign Relations (CFR) from where almost all the Presidents of the USA and their top aides have been chosen since the 1920s played a major role in the establishment of the United Nations in 1945. The Rockefellors(co-founders of CFR) meanwhile financed the headquarters of the League of Nations at Geneva, and later offered the land for building the UN head-quarters in New York. And CFR is believed to be subordinate to the RIIA in London; and such is the importance of the RIIA in global affairs.

The Astor family is one of the founders and financial backers of the RIIA and also one-time owners of the Times Newspapers. David Astor's progenitor John Jacob Astor was the wealthiest American in the 19th century, owning most of New York's Manhattan property. Another forefather Waldorf Astor of the Waldorf Astoria Hotel of New York, was the chairman of the RIIA, following the second world war. The Astors are also closely connected to the British Royal family.

Vaikuntha Vasan did not merely strike the iron while it was hot; but he also struck the nail on the right point; and lured the bird into the cage. Thereby, the Sri Lankan Tamil problem was also taken notice of at the highest levels-as that of the United Nations; of which more is dealt in Chapters 3 and 4...

Chapter 3

League of Nations to
The United Nations

All your strength is in your union,
All your danger is in discord.
-Longfellow

The United Nations is today the most prominent apex organisation of the world. Therefore the ensuing two chapters will beam suitable focus - firstly on the origins, aims and composition of the United Nations; followed by an insight into the leadership, operating mechanisms and actions performed within; and by allied organisations alongside this Institution.

The League of Nations

The forerunner of the United Nations was the League of Nations, the first international organisation that came into being, "to promote international cooperation and to achieve peace and security." The American President Woodrow Wilson advised by Bernard Baruch and Col. Mandel House (Round Table), propounded the "Fourteen Points" plan for world peace on Jan 8, 1918; with a view to bring an end to the First World War, that had ravaged Europe. Woodrow Wilson was honoured with the Nobel Peace Prize in 1919 for his initiative. The crux of the Fourteen Points Plan were: Facilitate free and open negotiations between nations; Reduction of weapons of war; Encourage free trade; Protect the freedom of the seas, Restoration of lands occupied by Germany, including returning of Alsace-Lorraine to France, and the establishment of the **League of Nations.**

The official end of the First World War came with the Versailles Peace Conference held in the Palace of Versailles (Chateau de Versailles) near Paris. The League of Nations was thus established in 1919 under the Treaty of Versailles. The International Labour Organization (ILO) was also created under the Treaty of Versailles as an affiliated agency of the League. The headquarters of the League of Nations was moved to Geneva in 1920 (to a luxury hotel on the banks of Leman, later renamed as Palais Wilson). The Treaty of Lucarno signed in October 1925 reinforced the League's objectives. But Germany and Japan quit the League respectively in 1933 and 1935. The Japanese invasion of Manchuria and the Italian invasion of Ethiopia discredited the League as a peace- keeping organisation. After failing to prevent the Second World War, the League of Nations subsequently collapsed in 1945.

Birth of the United Nations

Representatives of 50 nations met in San Francisco in 1945, at the United Nations Conference on International Organization to draw up the United Nations Charter. Deliberating on the basis of the proposals worked out by the representatives of China, Soviet Union, UK, and USA at Dumbarton Oaks, USA in August-October 1944; the Delegates signed the Charter on 26th June 1945. The United Nations officially came into existence on 24 October 1945. With the subsequent signing up by Poland, the original Member States of the United Nations stood at 51. The total number of Member States in May 2002 is now 191 (*see Table on pages 40-45).*

International Organizations were first established to cooperate on specific matters. The first such Institution -The International Telecommunication Union was founded in 1865 as the International Telegraph Union; and later the Universal Postal Union was established in 1874. The first International Peace Conference was held in The Hague, in the spot where the present International Peace Palace has been built; to elaborate instruments for settling crises peacefully, preventing wars and codifying rules of warfare.

US President Franklin Roosevelt coined the name: "United Nations"in consultations with Winston Churchill; and it was first used in the "Declaration by United Nations" of 1 January 1942, during the second world war, when representatives of 26 Nations pledged their governments to continue fighting together against the Axis Powers (Germany, Japan, Italy).

United Nations Charter

The Charter of the United Nations is the constituting apparatus of the Organization, setting out the rights and obligations of Member States, and establishing the United Nations organs and procedures. It is an international treaty. The Charter codifies the major principles of international relations; from the sovereign equality of States - to the prohibition of the use of force in international relations.

Preamble to the United Nations Charter

The Preamble to the United Nations Charter 1945, expresses

as follows the ideals and common aims of all the peoples whose governments joined together to form the United Nations: "WE THE PEOPLE OF THE UNITED NATIONS DETERMINED to save succeeding generations from the scourge of war, which twice in our lifetime has brought untold sorrow to mankind and to reaffirm faith in fundamental human rights, in the dignity and worth of the human person, in the equal rights of men and women and of nations large and small, and to establish conditions under which justice and respect for the obligations arising from treaties and other sources of international law can be maintained, and to promote social progress and better standards of life in larger freedom, AND FOR THESE ENDS to practice tolerance and live together in peace with one another as good neighbours and to unite our strength to maintain international peace and security, and to ensure, by the acceptance of principles and the institution of methods, that armed force shall not be used, save in the common interest, and to employ international machinery for the promotion of the economic and social advancement of all peoples, HAVE RESOLVED TO COMBINE OUR EFFORTS TO ACCOMPLISH THESE AIMS. Accordingly, our respective Governments, through representatives assembled in the city of San Francisco, who have exhibited their full powers found to be in good and due form, have agreed to the present Charter of the United Nations and do hereby establish an international organization to be known as the United Nations."

Purposes and Principles of the United Nations
Purposes

    1. To maintain international peace and security.
    2. To develop friendly relations among nations based

on respect for the principle of equal rights and self-determination of peoples.

3. To cooperate in solving international economic, social, cultural and humanitarian problems and in promoting respect for human rights and fundamental freedoms.

4. To be a centre for harmonizing the actions of nations in attaining these common ends.

Principles

1. It is based on the sovereign equality of all its Members;
2. All Members are to fulfil in good faith their Charter obligations;
3. They are to settle their international disputes by peaceful means and without endangering interna tional peace and security, and justice;
4. They are to refrain from the threat or use of force against any other state;
5. They are to give the United Nations every assistance in any action it takes in accordance with the Charter;
6. Nothing in the Charter is to authorize the United Nations to intervene in matters, which are essentially within the domestic jurisdiction of any state.

Membership

Membership of the United Nations is open to all peace-loving nations, which accept the obligations of the Charter and are willing and able to carry out these obligations.

The General Assembly admits new Member States on the recommendation of the Security Council. Even though the Charter
provides for the suspension or expulsion of a Member for vio-
lation of the principles of the Charter, no such action has ever
been taken to date.

Official languages
Under the Charter, the official languages of the United Nations
are Chinese, English, French, Russian and Spanish. Arabic has
been added as an official language of the General Assembly, the
Security Council and the Economic and Social Council.

Structure of the Organization
The Charter established six principal organs of the United
Nations which are the; (1) General Assembly (2) Security
Council (3) Economic and Social Council (4) Trusteeship
Council (5) International Court of Justice and (6) the
Secretariat. The United Nations family, however, is much larg-
er, encompassing 15 agencies and several programmes and
bodies.

(1) General Assembly
The General Assembly is the main deliberative organ. It is composed of representatives of all Member States, each of which
has one vote. Decisions on important questions, such as those
on peace and security, admission of new Members and budgetary matters, require a two-thirds majority. Decisions on other
questions are by simple majority.

Functions and powers
The functions and powers of the General Assembly are:

1. To consider and make recommendations on the principles
   of cooperation in the maintenance of international peace
   and security, including the principles governing disarma-

ment and arms regulation;

2. To discuss any question relating to international peace and security and, except where a dispute or situation is being discussed by the Security Council, to make recommendations on it;

3. To discuss and, with the same exception, make recommendations on any question within the scope of the Charter or affecting the powers and functions of any organ of the United Nations;

4. To initiate studies and make recommendations to promote international political cooperation, the development and cod ification of international law, the realization of human rights and fundamental freedoms for all, and international collaboration in economic, social, cultural, educational and health fields;

5. To make recommendations for the peaceful settlement of any situation, regardless of origin, which might impair friendly relations among nations;

6. To receive and consider reports from the Security Council and other United Nations organs;

7. To consider and approve the United Nations budget and to apportion the contributions among Members;

8. To elect the non-permanent members of the Security Council, the members of the Economic and Social Council and those members of the Trusteeship Council that are elected; to elect jointly with the Security Council the Judges of the International Court of Justice; and, on the recommendation of the Security Council, to appoint the Secretary-General.

Assembly Sessions

The General Assembly's regular session usually begins each year in September. The 2002-2003 session, for example, is the fifty-seventh regular session of the General Assembly. At the start of each regular session, the Assembly elects a new

President, 21 Vice-Presidents and the Chairpersons of the Assembly's six Main Committees. To ensure equitable geographical representation, the presidency of the Assembly rotates each year among five groups of states; African, Asian, Eastern European, Latin American and the Caribbean, and Western European and other states.

In addition, the Assembly may meet in special sessions at the request of the Security Council, of a majority of Member States, or of one Member if the majority of Members concur. Emergency special sessions may be called within 24 hours of a request by the Security Council on the vote of any nine Council members, or by a majority of the United Nations Members, or by one Member if the majority of Members concur.

At the beginning of each regular session, the Assembly holds a general debate, often addressed by heads of state and government, in which Member States express their views on the most pressing international issues. Most questions are then discussed in its six Main Committees:

1. First Committee (Disarmament and International Security);
2. Second Committee (Economic and Financial);
3. Third Committee (Social, Humanitarian and Cultural);
4. Fourth Committee (Special Political and De-colonization);
5. Fifth Committee (Administrative and Budgetary);
6. Sixth Committee (Legal).

Some issues are considered only in plenary meetings, rather than in one of the Main Committees. All issues are voted on through resolutions passed in plenary meetings, usually towards the end of the regular session, after the committees have completed their consideration of them and submitted draft resolutions to the plenary Assembly.

Voting in committees is by simple majority. In plenary meetings, resolutions may be adopted by acclamation, without objection or without a vote, or the vote may be recorded or taken by roll call.

While the decisions of the Assembly have no legally binding force for governments, they carry the weight of world opinion, as well as the moral authority of the world community.

The work of the United Nations year-round derives largely from the decisions of the General Assembly – that is to say, the will of the majority of the Members as expressed in resolutions adopted by the Assembly. That work is carried out:

1. By committees and other bodies established by the Assembly to study and report on specific issues, such as disarmament, peace keeping, development and human rights;
2. International conferences called for by the Assembly; and
3. By the Secretariat of the United Nations - the Secretary General and his staff of international civil servants.

(2) Security Council

Under the United Nations Charter, the Security Council has primary responsibility for the maintenance of international peace and security.

The Security Council has 15 members; 5 permanent members – China, France, the Russian Federation, the United Kingdom and the United States – and 10 elected by the General Assembly for two-year terms. Each member has one vote. Decisions on procedural matters are made by an affirmative vote of at least 9 of the 15 members. Decisions on substantive matters require nine votes, including the concurring votes of all five permanent members. This is the rule of "great Power unanimity", often referred to as the "veto" power. If a permanent member does not agree with a decision, it can cast a negative vote and this act has power of veto. All five permanent members have exercised the right of veto at one time or another. If a permanent member does not fully agree with a decision but does not wish to cast its veto, it may abstain.

Under the Charter, all Members of the United Nations agree to accept and carry out the decisions of the Security Council. While other organs of the United Nations make recommendations to governments, the Council alone has the power to take decisions, which Member States are obligated under the Charter to carry out.

Functions and powers
The functions and powers of the Security Council are:

1. To maintain international peace and security in accordance with the principles and purposes of the United Nations;
2. To investigate any dispute or situation which might lead to international friction;
3. To recommend methods of adjusting such disputes or the terms of settlement;
4. To formulate plans for establishing a system to regulate armaments;
5. To determine the existence of a threat to the peace or act of aggression and to recommend what action should be taken;
6. To call on Members to apply economic sanctions and other measures not involving the use of force to prevent or stop aggression;
7. To take military action against an aggressor;
8. To recommend the admission of new Members;

9. To exercise the trusteeship functions of the United Nations in "strategic areas";
10. To recommend to the General Assembly the appointment of the Secretary-General and, together with the Assembly, to elect the judges of the International Court of Justice.

The Security Council is so organized as to be able to function continuously, and a representative of each of its members must be present at all times at United Nations Headquarters. The Council may meet elsewhere: in 1972, it held a session in Addis Ababa, Ethiopia; in 1973 it met in Panama City, Panama; and in 1990 it met in Geneva, Switzerland.

When a complaint concerning a threat to peace is brought before it, the Security Council's first action is usually to recommend that the parties try to reach agreement by peaceful means. The Council may set forth principles for a peaceful settlement. In some cases, the Council itself undertakes investigation and mediation. It may dispatch a mission, appoint special representatives or request the Secretary – General to use his good offices.

When a dispute leads to fighting, the Security Council's first concern is to bring it to an end as soon as possible. The Council may issue ceasefire directives that can be instrumental in preventing wider hostilities.

The Security Council may also dispatch military observers or a peace - keeping force to help reduce tensions, keep opposing forces apart and create conditions of calm in which peaceful settlements may be sought. Under Chapter VII of the Charter, the Council may decide on enforcement measures, including economic sanctions (such as trade embargoes), arms embargoes or collective military action.

A working group of the General Assembly has been considering the reform of the Security Council since 1993, including equitable representation and expansion of membership.

(3) Economic and Social Council

The Charter established the Economic and Social Council as the principal organ to coordinate the economic, social, and related work of the United Nations family of organizations. The council has 54 members, who serve for three-year terms. Voting in the Council is by simple majority; each member has one vote.

Functions and powers

The functions and powers of the Economic and Social Council are:

1. To serve as the central forum for discussing international economic and social issues, and for formulating policy recommendations addressed to Member States and the United Nations system;
2. To make or initiate studies and reports and make recomendations on international economic, social, cultural, educa - tional, health and related matters;
3. To promote respect for, and observance of, human rights and fundamental freedoms;
4. To assist in preparing and organizing major international conferences in the economic, social and related fields and promote a co-ordinated follow-up to these conferences;

5. To coordinate the activities of the specialized agencies, through consultations with and recommendations to them, and through recommendations to the General Assembly.

Through its discussion of international economic and social issues and its policy recommendations, ECOSOC plays a key role in fostering international cooperation for development and in setting the priorities for action.

Sessions

The Economic and Social Council generally holds several short sessions throughout the year to deal with the organization of its work, as well as one four-week substantive session in July, alternating between New York and Geneva. The session includes a high-level segment, attended by Ministers and other high officials, to discuss major economic, social and humanitarian issues. The year-round work of the Council is carried out in its subsidiary and related bodies.

Subsidiary and related bodies
The Economic and Social Council's subsidiary machinery includes:

1. Nine functional commissions, which are deliberative bodies whose role is to consider and make recommendations on issues in their areas of responsibility and expertise: (1) Statistical Commission, (2) Commission on Population and Development, (3) Commission for Social Development (4) Commission on Human Rights, (5) Commission on the Status of Women, (6) Commission on Narcotic Drugs, (7) Commission on Crime Prevention and Criminal Justice, (8)Commission on Science and Technology for Development and (9) Commission on Sustainable Development.

2. Five Regional Commissions: (1) Economic Commission for Africa (Addis Ababa, Ethiopia) (2) Economic and Social Commission for Asia and the Pacific (Bangkok, Thailand) (3) Economic Commission for Europe (Geneva, Switzerland) (4) Economic Commission for Latin America and the Caribbean (Santiago, Chile) and (5) Economic and Social Commission for Western Asia (Beirut, Lebanon).

3. Five standing committees and expert bodies: (1) Committee for Programme and Coordination, (2) Commission on Human Settlements, (3) Committee on Non-Governmental Organizations, (4) Committee on Negotiations with Intergovernmental Agencies and (5) Committee on Energy and Natural Resources;

4. A number of expert bodies on subjects such as development planning, natural resources, and economic, social and cultural rights.

The Council also cooperates with and to a certain extent coordinates the work of United Nations programmes (such as UNDP, UNEP, UNICEF and UNFPA) and the specialized agencies (such as FAO, WHO, ILO and UNESCO), all of which report to the Council and make recommendations for its substantive sessions.

Relations with non-governmental organizations

Under the Charter, the Economic and Social Council consults with non-governmental organizations (NGOs) concerned with matters within its competence. Over 1,600 NGO's have consultative status with the Council. The Council recognizes that these organizations should have the opportunity to express their views, and that they possess special experience or technical knowledge of value to its work.

The Council classifies NGOs into three categories: category I organizations are those concerned with most of the Council's activities; category II organizations have special competence in specific areas; and organizations that can occasionally contribute to the Council are placed on a roster for ad hoc consultations.

NGOs with consultative status may send observers to meetings of the Council and its subsidiary bodies and may submit written statements relevant to its work. They may also consult with the United Nations Secretariat on matters of mutual concern.

Over the years, the relationship between the United Nations and affiliated NGOs has developed significantly. Increasingly NGOs are seen as partners who are consulted on policy and programme matters and seen as valuable links to civil society. NGOs around the world, in increasing numbers, are working daily with the United Nations community to help achieve the objectives of the Charter.

Trusteeship Council

The Trusteeship Council was established by the Charter in 1945 to provide international supervision for 11 Trust Territories placed under the administration of 7 Member States, and ensure that adequate steps were taken to prepare the Territories for self-government or independence. The Charter authorized the Trusteeship Council to examine and discuss reports from the Administering Authority on the political, economic, social and educational advancement of the peoples of Trust Territories; to examine petitions from the Territories; and to undertake special missions to the Territories.

By 1994, all Trust Territories had attained self-government or independence, either as separate States or by joining neighbouring independent countries. The last to do so was the Trust Territory of the Pacific Islands (Palau), which became the 185th Member State. Its work completed, the Trusteeship Council-consisting of the five permanent members of the Security Council, China, France, the Russian Federation, the United Kingdom and the United States – has amended its rules of procedure to meet as and where occasion may require.

International Court of Justice

Located at The Hague, the Netherlands, the International Court of Justice is the principal judicial organ of the United Nations. It settles legal disputes between states and gives advisory opinions to the United Nations and its specialized agencies. Its Statute is an integral part of the United Nations Charter. The Court is open to all states that are parties to its Statute, which include all Members of the United Nations and Switzerland. Only states may be parties in contentious cases before the Court and submit disputes to it. The Court is not open to private persons and entities or international organizations. The General Assembly and the Security Council can ask the Court for an advisory opinion on any legal question. Other organs of the United Nations and the specialized agencies, when authorized by the Assembly, can ask for advisory opinons on legal questions within the scope of their activities.

Jurisdiction

The Court's jurisdiction covers all questions that states refer to it, and all matters provided for in the United Nations Charter, or in international treaties and conventions. States may bind them selves in advance to accept the jurisdiction of the Court, either by signing a treaty or convention that provides for referral to the Court or by making a declaration to that effect. Such declarations accepting compulsory jurisdiction often contain reservations excluding certain classes of disputes.

In accordance with its Statute, the Court decides disputes by applying:
1. **International conventions establishing rules expressly recognized by the contesting states;**
2. **International custom as evidence of a general practice accepted as law;**
3. **The general principles of law recognized by nations; and**
4. **Judicial decisions and the teachings of the most qualified scholars of the various nations.**

Membership

The Court is comprised of 15 Judges elected by the General Assembly and the Security Council, voting independently. They are chosen on the basis of their qualifications, and care is taken to ensure that the principal legal systems of the world are represented in the Court. No two Judges may be from the same country. The Judges serve for a nine-year term and may be re-elected. They cannot engage in any other occupation during their term of office. The Court normally sits in plenary session, but may form smaller units called chambers if the parties so request. Judgments given by chambers are considered as rendered by the full Court. The Court also has a Chamber for

Environmental Matters and forms annually a Chamber of
Summary Procedure.

Secretariat

The Secretariat – an international staff working in duty stations
around the world – carries out the diverse day-to day work of
the Organization. It services the other principal organs of the
United Nations and administers the programmes and policies
laid down by them. At its head is the Secretary-General, who is
appointed by the General Assembly on the recommendation of
the Security Council for a five-year, renewable term.

The duties carried out by the Secretariat are as varied as the
problems dealt with by the United Nations. These range from
administering peacekeeping operations to mediating international disputes, from surveying economic and social trends to
preparing studies on human rights and sustainable development. Secretariat staff also informs the world's communications
media about the work of the United Nations; organize international conferences on issues of worldwide concern; and inter-
pret speeches and translate documents into the Organization's
official languages.

The Secretariat has a staff of about 8,900 under the regular
budget, drawn from 160 countries. As international civil servants, staff members and the Secretary-General answer to the
United Nations alone for their activities, and take an oath not to
seek or receive instructions from any government or outside
authority. Under the Charter, each Member State undertakes to
respect the exclusively international character of the responsibilities of the Secretary-General and the staff, and to refrain
from seeking to influence them improperly.The United Nations
while headquartered in New York, maintains a significant presence in Addis Ababa, Bangkok, Beirut, Geneva, Nairobi

Santiago and Vienna, and has offices all over the world.

Secretary-General

Equal parts diplomat and advocate, civil servant and CEO; the Secretary-General is a symbol of United Nations ideals and a spokesman for the interests of the world's peoples, in particular the poor and vulnerable. The current Secretary-General, and the seventh occupant of the post, is Mr. Kofi Annan, of Ghana, who took office on 1 January 1997.

The Charter describes the Secretary-General as "chief administrative officer" of the Organization, who shall act in that capacity and perform "such other functions as are entrusted" to him or her by the Security Council, General Assembly, Economic and Social Council and other United Nations organs. The Charter also empowers the Secretary-General to "bring to the attention of the Security Council any matter which in his opinion may threaten the maintenance of international peace and security". These guidelines both define the powers of the office and grant it considerable scope for action. The Secretary-General would fail if he did not take careful account of the concerns of Member States, but he must also uphold the values and moral authority of the United Nations, and speak and act for peace, even at the risk, from time to time, of challenging or dis agreeing with those same Member States.

This creative tension accompanies the Secretary-General through day-to-day work, which includes attendance at sessions of United Nations bodies; consultations with world leaders, government officials and others; and worldwide travel intended to keep him in touch with the peoples of Member States and informed about the vast array of issues of international concern that are on the Organization's agenda. Each year, the Secretary-

General issues a report on the work of the Organization that appraises its activities and outlines future priorities.

One of the most vital roles played by the Secretary-General is the use of his "good offices" – steps taken publicly and in private, drawing upon his independence, impartiality and integrity, to prevent international disputes from arising, escalating or spreading. Each Secretary-General also defines his role during and within the context of his particular time in office.

Deputy Secretary-General

A new post of Deputy Secretary-General was created to assist the Secretary-General in the array of responsibilities assigned to his office. Ms. Louise Frechette, former Deputy Minister of National Defence of Canada, has been appointed as the new Deputy Secretary-General from 1998.

Budget of the United Nations

The General Assembly approves the Budget of the United Nations every two years. It is submitted by the Secretary-General and reviewed by an Advisory Committee made up of experts. The budget approved for the two years 2000-2001, for example, was $2,535million. The main source of funds for the budget is the contributions of Member States, as assessed on a scale approved by the General Assembly on the recommendations of the Committee on Contributions. The scale is based upon the capacity of countries' ability to pay by taking into consideration the relative shares of total gross national product and their per capita incomes. In year 2000, the General assembly fixed a maximum of 22% of the budget from any one contributor. This was obviously intended to limit the contribution of a large and wealthy country, like the USA, to a maximum of 22%, so as to preserve the independence of the UN. Despite the failure of Member States to pay their dues in full and on time, the United Nations has managed to continue to operate through generous voluntary contributions from some countries. Also its Working Capital Fund, made up from advances from Member Sates, and borrowings from peacekeeping operations has come in good use for the World Body.

Further to the above, the United Nations funds and programmes such as UNICEF, UNDP etc. and all the United Nations specialized agencies such as ILO, FAO, IMF etc. have separate and larger budgets, met with voluntary contributions from Member States.

The United Nations Family

The United Nations Family of Organizations otherwise called the United Nations system composed of (1) United Nations Secretariat (2) UN Programmes and Funds (such as UNICEF, UNDP) and (3) Specialized Agencies (such as ILO, FAO, IMF) - all coherently and actively play the global role of maintaining peace and progress in an era of momentous transition and transformation.

The Security Council has established two International Criminal Tribunals to prosecute crimes against humanity in the former Yugoslavia and in Rwanda. The Tribunals are subsidiary organs of the Council. Post-Gulf war, to verify the elimination of Iraq's weapons of mass destruction, the Security Council established the United Nations Special Commission (UNSCOM). Its responsibilities have been taken over by the United Nations Monitoring, Verification and Inspection Commission ((UNMOVIC), which the Council established in 2000.

A Comprehensive List of Members of the United Nations as at May 2002 (Estimated Populations 1998-2000) is presented in the following pages:

United Nations Members List

Member State	Date of Admission	Population (est)
Afghanistan	19 November 1946	21,400,000
Albania	14 December 1955	3,791,000
Algeria	8 October 1962	29,800,000
Andorra	28 July 1993	72,000
Angola	1 December 1976	12,092,000
Antigua and Barbuda	11 November 1981	67,000
Argentina	24 October 1945	36,125,000
Armenia	2 March 1992	3,536,000
Australia	1 November 1945	18,750,000
Austria	14 December 1955	8,077,000
Azerbaijan	2 March 1992	7,953,000
Bahamas	18 September 1973	298,000
Bahrain	21 September 1971	642,000
Bangladesh	17 September 1974	124,774,000
Barbados	9 December 1966	266,000
Belarus	24 October 1945	10,190,000
Belgium	27 December 1945	10,213,000
Belize	25 September 1981	238,000
Benin	20 September 1960	6,044,000
Bhutan	21 September 1971	2,004,000
Bolivia	14 November 1945	7,949,000
Bosnia and Herzegovina	22 May 1992	4,211,000
Botswana	17 October 1966	1,571,000
Brazil	24 October 1945	161,790,000
Brunei Darussalam	21 September 1984	315,000
Bulgaria	14 December 1955	8,256,000
Burkina Faso	20 September 1960	10,682,000
Burundi	18 September 1962	6,300,000
Cambodia	14 December 1955	11,426,000
Cameroon	20 September 1960	14,305,000
Canada	9 November 1945	30,301,000
Cape Verde	16 September 1975	417,000
Central African Republic	20 September 1960	3,485,000

Member State	Date of Admission	Population(est)
Chad	20 September 1960	7,270,000
Chile	24 October 1945	14,821,000
China	24 October 1945	1,255,698,000
Colombia	5 November 1945	40,826,000
Comoros	12 November 1975	658,000
Congo	20 September 1960	2,785,000
Costa Rica	2 November 1945	3,340,000
Cote d'Ivoire	20 September 1960	14,292,000
Croatia	22 May 1992	4,572,000
Cuba	24 October 1945	11,116,000
Cyprus	20 September 1960	749,000
Czech Republic	19 January 1993	10,294,000
Democratic People's Republic of Korea	17 September 1991	23,348,000
Democratic Republic Of the Congo	20 September 1960	46,812,000
Denmark	24 October 1945	5,301,000
Djibouti	20 September 1977	623,000
Dominica	18 December 1978	71,000
Dominican Republic	24 October 1945	9,327,000
East Timor	May 2002	750,000
Ecuador	21 December 1945	12,174,000
Egypt	24 October 1945	65,978,000
El Salvador	24 October 1945	6,031,000
Equatorial Guinea	12 November 1968	431,000
Eritrea	28 May 1993	3,577,000
Estonia	17 September 1991	1,429,000
Ethiopia	13 November 1945	59,882,000
Federated States of Micronesia	17 September 1991	114,000
Fiji	13 October 1970	796,000
Finland	14 December 1955	5,154,000
France	24 October 1945	58,846,000
Gabon	20 September 1960	1,188,000
Gambia	21 September 1965	1,229,000
Georgia	31 July 1992	5,059,000
Germany	18 September 1973	82,024,000

Members State	Date of Admission	Population(est
Ghana	8 March 1957	19,162,000
Greece	25 October 1945	10,515,000
Grenada	17 September 1974	93,000
Guatemala	21 November 1945	10,799,000
Guinea	12 December 1958	7,337,000
Guinea-Bissau	17 September 1974	1,161,000
Guyana	20 September 1966	850,000
Haiti	24 October 1945	7,647,000
Honduras	17 December 1945	6,179,000
Hungary	14 December 1955	10,113,000
Iceland	19 November 1946	273,000
India	30 October 1945	970,933,000
Indonesia	28 September 1950	204,392,000
Iran (Islamic Republic of)	24 October 1945	61,626,000
Iraq	21 December 1945	21,800,000
Ireland	14 December 1955	3,705,000
Israel	11 May 1949	5,963,000
Italy	14 December 1955	57,588,000
Jamaica	18 September 1962	2,576,000
Japan	18 December 1956	126,410,000
Jordan	14 December 1955	6,304,000
Kazakhstan	2 March 1992	15,049,000
Kenya	16 December 1963	29,008,000
Kiribati	14 September1999	81,000
Kuwait	14 May 1963	2,027,000
Kyrgyzstan	2 March 1992	4,699,000
Lao People's Democratic Republic	14 December 1955	5,163,000
Latvia	17 September 1991	2,449,000
Lebanon	24 October 1945	3,191,000
Lesotho	17 October 1966	2,062,000
Liberia	2 November 1945	2,700,000
Libyan Arab Jamahiriya	14 December 1955	5,339,000
Liechtenstein	18 September 1990	32,000
Lithuania	17 September 1991	3,700,000
Luxembourg	24 October 1945	426,000
Madagascar	20 September 1960	15,057,000

Member State	Date of Admission	Population (est)
Malawi	1 December 1964	10,346,000
Malaysia	17 September 1957	22,179,000
Maldives	21 September 1965	271,000
Mali	28 September 1960	10,694,000
Malta	1 December 1964	377,000
Marshall Islands	17 September 1991	63,000
Mauritania	27 October 1961	2,529,000
Mauritius	24 April 1968	1,159,000
Mexico	7 November 1945	95,831,000
Monaco	28 May 1993	33,000
Mongolia	27 October 1961	2,403,000
Morocco	12 November 1956	27,775,000
Mozambique	16 September 1975	17,796,000
Myanmar	19 April 1948	44,497,000
Namibia	23 April 1990	1,666,000
Nauru	14 September 1999	11,000
Nepal	14 December 1955	22,800,000
Netherlands	10 December 1945	15,707,000
New Zealand	24 October 1945	3,790,000
Nicaragua	24 October 1945	4,807,000
Niger	20 September 1960	10,078,000
Nigeria	7 October 1960	106,409,000
Norway	27 November 1945	4,431,000
Oman	7 October 1971	2,287,000
Pakistan	30 September 1947	148,166,000
Palau	15 December 1994	19,000
Panama	13 November 1945	2,763,000
Papua New Guinea	10 October 1975	4,600,000
Paraguay	24 October 1945	5,218,000
Peru	31 October 1945	24,800,000
Philippines	24 October 1945	75,154,000
Poland	24 October 1945	38,671,000
Portugal	14 December 1955	9,957,000
Qatar	21 September 1971	543,000
Republic of Korea	17 September 1991	46,429,000
Republic of Moldova	2 March 1992	4,237,000
Romania	14 December 1955	22,502,000
Russian Federation	24 October 1945	147,739,000

Member State	Date of Admission	Population(est)
Rwanda	18 September 1962	6,604,000
Saint Kitts and Nevis	23 September 1983	39,000
Saint Lucia	18 September 1979	151,000
Saint Vincent and The Grenadines	16 September 1980	112,000
Samoa	15 December 1976	168,000
San Marino	2 March 1992	26,000
Sao Tome and Principe	16 September 1975	141,000
Saudi Arabia	24 October 1945	20,181,000
Senegal	28 September 1960	9,037,000
Seychelles	21 September 1976	78,000
Sierra Leone	27 September 1961	4,568,000
Singapore	21 September 1965	3,865,000
Slovakia	19 January 1993	5,390,000
Slovenia	22 May 1992	1,983,000
Solomon Islands	19 September 1978	417,000
Somalia	20 September 1960	9,237,000
South Africa	7 November 1945	39,357,000
Spain	14 December 1955	39,371,000
Sri Lanka	14 December 1955	18,774,000
Sudan	12 November 1956	28,292,000
Suriname	4 December 1975	414,000
Swaziland	24 September 1968	952,000
Sweden	19 November 1946	8,854,000
Switzerland	May 2002	7,400,000
Syrian Arab Republic	24 October 1945	15,597,000
Tajikistan	2 March 1992	6,103,000
Thailand	16 December 1946	61,201,000
The former Yugoslav Republic of Macedonia	8 April 1993	1,999,000
Togo	20 September 1960	4,397,000
Tonga	14 September 1999	98,000
Trinidad and Tobago	18 September 1962	1,283,000
Tunisia	12 November 1956	9,332,000
Turkey	24 October 1945	63,451,000
Turkmenistan	2 March 1992	4,858,000
Tuvalu	5 September 2000	10,000
Uganda	25 October 1962	21,029,000

Member State	Date of Admission	Population(est)
Ukraine	24 October 1945	50,499,000
United Arab Emirates	9 December 1971	2,274,000
United Kingdom	24 October 1945	58,649,000
United Republic of Tanzania	14 December 1961	32,102,000
United States of America	24 October 1945	270,561,000
Uruguay	18 December 1945	3,289,000
Uzbekistan	2 March 1992	24,050,000
Vanuatu	15 September 1981	182,000
Venezuela	15 November 1945	23,436,000
Viet Nam	20 September 1977	76,325,000
Yemen	30 September 1947	17,071,000
Yugoslavia	1 November 2000	10,615,000
Zambia	1 December 1964	8,781,000
Zimbabwe	25 August 1980	12,684,000

Chapter 4

Insight into the United Nations

A round up of the entire United Nations Organisation has been composed here for obtaining a proper perspective and insight into this mammoth international body.

United Nations Secretariat

The United Nations Secretariat consists of Departments and Offices. The Executive Office of the Secretary-General, composed of the Secretary-General and his senior advisers, establishes general policies, provides overall guidance, and controls the running of the Organization. The Secretariat has its headquarters in New York and subsidiary offices in all regions of the world, with the following immediate branches:

1. United Nations Office at Geneva (UNOG) – headed by Under-Secretary-General Vladimir Petrovsky (Russian Federation), specialising on Disarmament, Human Rights and Conference Diplomacy.

2. United Nations Office at Vienna (UNOV) – headed by Under-Secretary-General Pino Arlacchi (Italy), specialising on

International Trade Law, Outer Space, International Drug Abuse Control, Crime Prevention and Criminal Justice.
3. United Nations Office at Nairobi (UNON) – headed by Under-Secretary-General Klaus Topfer(Germany), specialising on Environment and Human Settlements.
It is especially interesting to have a penetrating over-view of this galactic Organisation in New York:

Office of Internal Oversight Services (OIOS)
Resembles an internal audit department in a corporate body; monitoring and evaluating implementation of programmes and mandates, investigating mismanagements and carrying out the internal audits and inspections.

Office of Legal Affairs (OLA)
The central legal service of the UN, provides legal advice from the Secretary-General down to all the organs of the UN. Also performs legal drafting function.

Department of Political Affairs (DPA)
Advises the Secretary-General and also the Security Council on all political matters towards the maintenance and restoration of peace and security throughout the world. By providing consultations and negotiations relating to peaceful settlement of disputes, the focal point of this department enables the UN to perform peace-building and undertake preventive actions.

Department for Disarmament Affairs (DDA)
Promotes the goal of disarmament and non-proliferation of weapons of mass destruction such as - nuclear, chemical and

biological; and also of conventional weapons especially -landmines and small arms. Additionally, disarming and demobilizing former combatants and assist them to reintegrate into civil societies.

Department of Peacekeeping Operations (DPKO)

The operational arm for all United Nations Peacekeeping Operations. From planning and methodologies to logistics support and resource management is directed by the DPKO. The Under-Secretary-General directs all peacekeeping operations on behalf of the Secretary-General.

Office for the Coordination of Humanitarian Affairs (OCHA)

Provides coordination to ensure all humanitarian assistance is supplied in response to emergencies and also advocates humanitarian issues with Security Council and other political organs.

Department of Economic and Social Affairs (DESA)

1. A broad range of socio-economic-environmental data and information are collected and processed to advise member states to take stock of policy options.
2. Facilitates negotiations in intergovernmental bodies that meet in the UN and provide support to Member States on socio-economic-environmental issues.
3. Advises interested governments in ways and means of implementing policy frameworks that are agreed in conferences.

Department of General Assembly Affairs and Conference Services (DGAACS)

A Conference servicing department; provides technical and secretariat support services to the General assembly and all other bodies. Notable are the translation, documentation and publishing services.

Department of Public Information (DPI)
The DPI informs its global audience on the activities and purposes of the United Nations.
1. The Public Affairs Division conducts promotional information campaigns, and organizes special events, exhibitions, press conferences, workshops, special programmes and guided tours. It also serves as an information resource centre.
2. The News and Media Division communicates through: daily news via radio and internet; live TV feeds, press releases, video programming, and photo coverage of UN meetings and events.
3. The Library and Information Resources Division provides access through the Dag Hammarskjold Library, to UN documents and publications, both directly and through the internet and 350 depository libraries globally.
4. The Office of the Spokesman of the Secretary-General briefs journalists on a daily basis on behalf of the Secretary-General.

Department of Management (DM)
The Office of Programme Planning, Budget and Accounts; The Office of Human Resources Management, and the Office of Central Support Services respectively provide those services including policy formulation on those sectors to the UN.

Office of the Iraq Programme
Manages the "Oil for Food" programme, established by the Security Council in 1995 to provide to the humanitarian needs of the Iraqi people.

Office of the United Nations Security Coordinator (UNSECOORD)
Ensures that a coherent response is in operation in any emergency situation. Including the evacuation of UN staff and coordination of security and safety programmes. The above depart-

ments and offices thus comprise the set up in New York, the world headquarters of the United Nations.

The United Nations operate through a vast number of Organisations specialising in their own spheres. They are grouped here for clarity under: 1. Regional Commissions; 2. International Tribunals; 3. UN Programmes and allied Organisations; 4. Specialised Agencies and allied organisations; and 5. The World Bank Group.

1. Regional Commissions
Reporting to the Economic and Social Council, the United Nations Regional Commissions initiates measures to promote the economic development of each region.

1. Economic Commission for Africa (ECA)
    Office: *Addis Ababa, Ethiopia*
2..Economic Commission for Europe (ECE)
    Office: *Geneva, Switzerland*
3. Economic Commission for Latin America & the
    Caribbean(ECLAC)
    Office: *Santiago, Chile*
4. Economic and Social Commission for Asia and the Pacific
    (ESCAP)
    Office: *Bangkok, Thailand*
5. Economic and Social Commission for Western Asia
    (ESCWA)
    Office: *Beirut, Lebanon*

2. International Tribunals
International Criminal Tribunal for the Former Yugoslavia (ICTY)
Headquarters: *The Hague, the Netherlands*
Mandated to prosecute persons responsible for violations of serious international humanitarian law in the former Yugoslavia. Established in 1993 by the Security Council.

International Criminal Tribunal for Rwanda (ICTR)
Headquarters: *Arusha, Tanzania*
Created by the Security Council in 1994 to prosecute those responsible for genocide in Rwanda during 1994.

3. United Nations Programmes & allied Organisations
United Nations Conference on Trade and Development (UNCTAD)
Headquarters: *Geneva, Switzerland*
The principal organ of the General Assembly in the field of trade and development, it was established in 1964. UNCTAD's focal point is to maximise trade, investment and development opportunities of developing countries and help them face challenges arising from globalization.

International Trade Centre - UNCTAD/WTO (ITC)
Headquarters: *Geneva, Switzerland*
The technical operations agency of UNCTAD and the World Trade Organization(WTO); and a joint subsidiary of the UN and the WTO.

Office for Drug Control and Crime Prevention (ODCCP)
Headquarters: *Vienna, Austria*
Established in 1997 to enable the UN to enhance its capacity to handle the interrelated issues of drug control, crime prevention and international terrorism.

United Nations Environment Programme (UNEP)
Headquarters: *Nairobi, Kenya*
The principal UN body that sets the global environmental agenda; it was established in 1972.

United Nations Development Programme(UNDP)
Headquarters: *New York, USA*
The largest provider of development grant assistance(over $2

billions), the UNDP coordinates the UN Development Programme. The annual Human Development Report is one of its major publication.

United Nations Development Fund for Women (UNDFW)
Headquarters: *New York, USA*
Women's empowerment and gender equality are two important goals of UNDFW, which was established in 1976. It works through grass roots enterprises to improve women's working conditions and also designs new gender equality laws.

United Nations Volunteers (UNV)
Headquarters: *Bonn, Germany*
Created by the General Assembly in 1970, is a unique organ, for operating within the UN framework, and for its scale (average of 4,000 specialists/fieldworkers at any one time). It was also a focal point for the International Year of Volunteers 2001.

United Nations Population Fund (UNPF)
Headquarters :   *New York, USA*
As the largest internationally funded organisation for population control; UNPF assists countries to improve family planning and reproductive health, including HIV/AIDS and reduction of maternal mortality.

Office of the United Nations High Commissioner
for Refugees (UNHCR)
Headquarters: *Geneva, Switzerland*
With responsibility for *"international protection"* of refugees, this Office was created by the General Assembly in 1950, expecting a huge crisis in this respect. More than 5,000 work in 281 offices worldwide looking after over 21 million refugees. A two-yearly publication of UNHCR - *"The State of the World's Refugees"* gives a comprehensive analysis on the refugee crises.

United Nations Children's Fund (UNICEF)
Headquarters: *United Nations, New York*
Guided by the Convention on the Rights of the Child, the UNICEF is the only organization that is dedicated to uphold the rights and welfare of children. Established in 1946, the work of UNICEF covers 161 countries in the following ways: Prevention of childhood illnesses and death; making pregnancy and childbirth safe; enabling children to attend schools and also acquire skills;and providing emergency response in times of crisis. Over 5,000 staff with a budget of $1 billion strives to make the world a better place for children. In 1965 it was awarded the Nobel Peace Prize.

World Food Programme (WFP)
Headquarters: *Rome, Italy*
The food-aid arm of the United Nations system, WFP is the world's largest food-aid organization, established in 1963, mandated to help the poor in developing countries and combat world hunger and poverty. With a staff of over 5,000 (mostly temporary) the WFP provides fast, life-sustaining relief to victims of wars and natural and man-made disasters.

United Nations Relief and Works Agency for Palestinian Refugees in the Near East (UNRWA)
Headquarters: *Gaza City & Amman, Jordan*
Established following the 1948 Arab-Israel conflict, the UNRWA provide essential health, education, relief and social services to over 3.7 million Palestinian refugees scattered in the 59 refugee camps in the Middle East.

Office of the United Nations High Commissioner for Human Rights (OHCHR)
Headquarters: *Geneva, Switzerland*
Entrusted as the official principally responsible for United

Nations human rights activities, the United Nations High Commissioner for Human Rights is in charge of promoting and protecting the civil, cultural, economic, political, and social rights of all world citizens. Created by the General Assembly in 1993, the Office is organized into the following three branches: 1. Research and Right to Development Branch 2. Activities and Programme Branch and 3. Support Services Branch.

United Nations Centre for Human Settlements (Habitat)
Headquarters: *Nairobi, Kenya*
Habitat is the lead agency of the United Nations established in 1978 to coordinate and provide: 1. Shelter-for-all and 2. A Sustainable urban development programme. The Centre has published the Global Report on Human Settlements providing a complete review of human settlements conditions worldwide.

United Nations Office for Project Services (UNOPS)
Headquarters: *New York, USA*
The UN arm that manages a broad range of project services for developing countries.

United Nations University (UNU)
Headquarters: *Tokyo, Japan*
The United Nations University is an international community of scholars that acts as a bridge between the UN and the world academia; and functions as a Think-Tank, through research, postgraduate training and the dissemination of knowledge to further the United Nation's aims of: **1.**Peace **2.** Governance **3.** Development **4.** Environment **5.** Science, Technology and Society.

**Headquartered in Tokyo, the UNU has 13 centres through-
out the world, specialising in specific fields:**

1. UNU World Institute for Development Economics Research
   (UNU/WIDER), Helsinki, Finland.
2. UNU Institute for New Technologies (UNU/INTECH),
   Maastricht, the Netherlands.
3. UNU Institute for Natural Resources in Africa
   (UNU/INRA),   Accra, Ghana,
4. UNU International Institute for Software Technology
   UNU/IIST, Macau, China.
5. UNU Institute of Advanced Studies (UNU/IAS), Tokyo,
   Japan.
6. UNU Programme for Biotechnology in Latin America and
   the Caribbean (UNU/BIOLAC), Caracas, Venezuela.
7. UNU International Leadership Academy (UNU/ILA),
   Amman, Jordan.
8. UNU International Network on Water, Environment and
   Health (UNU/INWEH), Hamilton, Ontario, Canada.
9. UNU Food and Nutrition Programme for Human and Social
   Development, Ithaca, New York, United States.
10. UNU Geothermal Training Programme (UNU/GTP),
    Reykjavik, Iceland.
11. UNU Fisheries Training Programme (UNU/FTP),
    Reykjavik, Iceland.
12. Initiative on Conflict Resolution and Ethnicity(INCORE),
    Ulster, Northern Ireland, United Kingdom.
13. UNU Governance Programme (UNU/GP), Barcelona,
    Spain.

International Research and Training Institute for the Advancement of Women (INSTRAW)

Headquarters: *Dominican Republic*
Established following the recommendation of the first World
Conference on Women in 1976, INSTRAW has been uniquely
mandated to promote the advancement of women; including

their active and equal participation in the development process and gender equality programmes.

United Nations Interregional Crime and Justice Research Institute (UNICRI)

Headquarters :   *Turin, Italy*
Promotes and supports research and training to establish a reliable base of knowledge and information on organised crime. Through its international documentation centre on criminology, the Institute furthers the exchange of information between member countries.

United Nations Institute for Training and Research (UNITAR)

Headquarters: *Geneva, Switzerland*
An autonomous body mandated to boost the effectiveness of the United Nations through innovative training and research support to UN agencies, governments and NGOs. Through organized training and capacity building UNITAR endeavours to assist countries to meet the challenges of the 21st century.

United Nations Research Institute for Social Development (UNRISD)

Headquarters: *Geneva, Switzerland*
Another autonomous body, the UNRISD undertakes research on the social dimensions of problems affecting different social groups and of environmental changes affecting development policies.

United Nations Institute for Disarmament Research (UNIDIR)

Headquarters: *Geneva, Switzerland*
A contemporary Institute, with a small core of staff, undertakes research and conducts seminars on a wide range of disarma-

ment issues, from small arms to nuclear tactical weapons.

4. Specialized Agencies and allied Orgazations

International Labour Organization (ILO)
Headquarters: *Geneva, Switzerland*
Unique among the world organisations, the ILO is the eminent
agency that promotes labour rights and social justice. The first
specialised agency of the United Nations since 1946, but it was
established in 1919. It is composed of:

1. The International Labour Conference acting as a forum for
   governments, employers and workers to meet and set labour
   standards.
2. The ILO Governing Body directing ILO operations and
   examining cases of non-observance of ILO standards.
3. The International Labour Office acting as a permanent secretariat.

The ILO strives to improve working and labour conditions
worldwide and engages in research, education and training
through its Turin training centre in Italy. The Nobel Prize was
awarded to the ILO for its achievements in 1969, on its 50th
anniversary.

Food and Agriculture Organization of the United Nations (FAO)
Headquarters: *Rome, Italy*
Another jewel organisation decorating the UN crown, the FAO
is the paramount organisation promoting agricultural development; assisting nutritional improvement and ensuring food
security in the world. It endeavours to alleviate poverty and
hunger with its over 4,000 staff from its Rome head-quarters
and in the field around the world.

United Nations Educational, Scientific and Cultural Organization (UNESCO)

Headquarters: *Paris, France*

Headquartered in Paris, the cultural capital of the world, UNESCO was created in 1946, to enhance lasting peace through education, science and culture. The main objectives being: 1) Education for all 2) Environmental research through scientific programmes 3) Expression of cultural identities 4) Protection of natural and cultural heritages and 5) Promoting free flow of Information, Communication and Press Freedom. UNESCO has a staff of over 2,000; supported by 178 National commissions and 5,000 UNESCO Associations.

World Health Organization (WHO)

Headquarters: *Geneva, Switzerland*

Achievement of the highest possible level of health through the control and eradication of disease is the main objective of WHO. The World Health Assembly, composed of all the 193 member States, meets annually, to direct the WHO in the attainment of high quality of Life for humanity. With over 3,800 staff, there are regional offices in Brazzaville(Congo), Washington(USA), Cairo(Egypt), Copenhagen(Denmark), New Delhi(India), and Manila, Philippines.

International Civil Aviation Organization (ICAO)

Headquarters: *Montreal, Canada*

The ICAO set up in 1944 formulates international standards and regulations to provide for the safety, security, efficiency and regularity of air transport.

International Maritime Organization (IMO)

Headquarters: *London, England*

The IMO set up in 1959 is responsible for international maritime safety and prevention of pollution from ships. The IMO World Maritime University in Malmo, Sweden provides advanced training in shipping. The IMO International Maritime Law Institute in Valetta, Malta trains lawyers in international maritime law. The IMO International Maritime Academy in Trieste, Italy offers specialised maritime crash courses.

International Telecommunication Union (ITU)
Headquarters: *Geneva, Switzerland*
Founded in Paris in 1865 as the International Telegraphic Union; ITU changed to its present name in 1934 and became a UN specialised Agency in 1947. Governments and private telecom networks coordinate global telecommunication networks and services through this organisation.

Universal Postal Union (UPU)
Headquarters: *Berne, Switzerland*
Established under the Berne Treaty of 1874, UPU became a UN specialised agency in 1948. It is the primary organisation for cooperation between international postal services.

World Meteorological Organization (WMO)
Headquarters: *Geneva, Switzerland*
WMO provides reliable scientific information on atmospheric environment (applied meteorology, ozone layer depletion), climatic issues (tropical cyclones, El Nino, droughts, floods, global warming etc.) and Earth's freshwater resources(diminishing water resources).

World Intellectual Property Organization (WIPO)

Headquarters: *Geneva, Switzerland*
Established in 1970, WIPO promotes 1) Protection of industrial property (inventions, trademarks, industrial designs, and appellations of origins) through the 'Paris Union'-International Union for the Protection of Industrial Property. And 2) Protection of intellectual property (copyright of literary, musical, artistic, photographic and audiovisual works) through the Berne Union –the International Union for the Protection of Literary and Artistic Works.

International Fund for Agricultural Development (IFAD)

Headquarters: *Rome, Italy*
The IFAD set up in 1977 is a multilateral financial institution mandated to combat hunger and rural poverty., through mobilising funds for improved food production and better nutrition.

United Nations Industrial Development Organization (UNIDO)

Headquarters ·   *Vienna, Austria*
Established in 1966 to promote industrial development and cooperation; UNIDO offers tailor made solutions for sustainable industrial development for developing countries.

International Atomic Energy Agency (IAEA)

Headquarters: *Vienna, Austria*
The IAEA is the world's inspectorate for nuclear safety and a forum for scientific cooperation of peaceful uses of nuclear energy. It was set up in 1957. It also plays a vital role in international efforts aimed at preventing the proliferation of nuclear weapons.

Preparatory Commission for the Comprehensive Nuclear-Test-Ban Treaty Organization (CTBTO)

Headquarters: *Vienna, Austria*

The CTBTO was established on 19 November 1996 at a meeting in New York, of States Signatories to the Treaty, which banned any nuclear-test explosions anywhere.

Organisation for the Prohibition of Chemical Weapons (OPCW)

Headquarters: *The Hague, The Netherlands*

Following the Convention on the Prohibition of the development, production, stockpiling and use of chemical weapons; and of their destruction, the OPCW was established in 1977.

World Tourism Organization (WTO)

Headquarters: *Madrid, Spain*

World Tourism Organisation was established in 1925 to serve as a world body on tourism policy and for promoting and developing tourism.

World Trade Organization (WTO)

Headquarters: *Geneva, Switzerland*

The World Trade Organisation was established in 1995 to accelerate the process of globalisation; and thus replaced the General Agreement on Tariffs and Trade(GATT). WTO aims to promote a smooth flow of trade, based on rules, to promote free trade by reducing protectionism; And to encourage competition.

Specialised group of Agencies, the World Bank Group is the most influential organ in the UN Diaspora, deciding the economic fate of Nations and their people.

5. World Bank Group

Headquarters: *Washington, USA*

Improving of people's living standards through promoting economic growth and development around world is the chief objective of the World Bank group. The World Bank as its popularly known, with 11,000 staff and an annual budget of $1.4 billion, is composed of five Institutions as follows:

International Bank for Reconstruction and Development (IBRD)

Founded in 1946, following the Bretton Woods Conference of 1944, the IBRD provides loans and development assistance mainly to developing countries. Voting power is directly linked to member countries' capital subscriptions, thus the economically stronger members controlling the decision making process. With $11 billion of membership contributions, the IBRD had leveraged to raise $270 billion, through the sale of Bonds in International Capital Markets, which in turn has been loaned to developing economies.

International Development Association (IDA)

The IDA is the agency of the World Bank that provides long-term(35-40 years), interest free credit lines to the poorest countries (with annual per capita income of less than $895). The loans are provided for basic needs of the poorest members, such as elementary health, clean water, and sanitation, primary education, and environment protection; and also for liberalisation through private businesses. Contributions to funding is received mainly from the richer IDA members.

International Finance Corporation (IFC)

The IFC is the largest financial institution in the developing world, providing equity finance and loans for private-sector projects. And plays a catalytic role by complementing existing market investors; stimulating the governments to let a free flow of both domestic and international capital; and also through mobilisation of funds to let private investments prove to be profitable.

Multilateral Investment Guarantee Agency (MIGA)
The MIGA is purely an Insurance agency of the World Bank providing guarantees to foreign private investors against non-commercial political risks such as: war and civil disturbances, currency transfer and expropriation disputes. As such it fills into a void that the commercial insurance sector does not address.

International Centre for Settlement of Investment Disputes (ICSID)
The ICSID, an autonomous organization within the World Bank group, was established under the Convention on the Settlement of Investment Disputes between States of Nationals of Other States in 1966. And provides services through conciliation and arbitration between governments and the private foreign investors.

International Monetary Fund (IMF)
Headquarters   *Washington, USA*
Established at the Bretton Woods Conference in 1944, IMF is one of the more known UN institutions; providing temporary credits to members experiencing balance of payments difficul-ties. The primary subscription by all the member countries cur-rently total to about US$ 300 billions. IMF also has powers to create and allocate international finance in the form of "Special Drawing Rights"(SDRs). IMF often dictates economic policies on developing countries under the pretext of structural adjust-ments, which have only made poor countries into a state of never ending socio-economic crises.

And so we conclude a comprehensive survey of the UN Organisation.

Vaikuntha Vasan qualified as a Barrister on 17th May 1960. A Photographic portrait on being Called to the Bar in London.

Below:
Vaikuntha Vasan being feted by the Judicial Service colleagues when he served as a Magistrate in Zambia.
He is seen here with Titus Mapani, a senior Judicial Service Official of Zambia.

Right:
Vaikuntha
Vasans pose
on their wed-
ding day, 15th
May 1945.

Below:
The proud pro-
genitors of
Vaikuntha
Vasan, left:
father Krishna
and right:
mother
Lakshmi

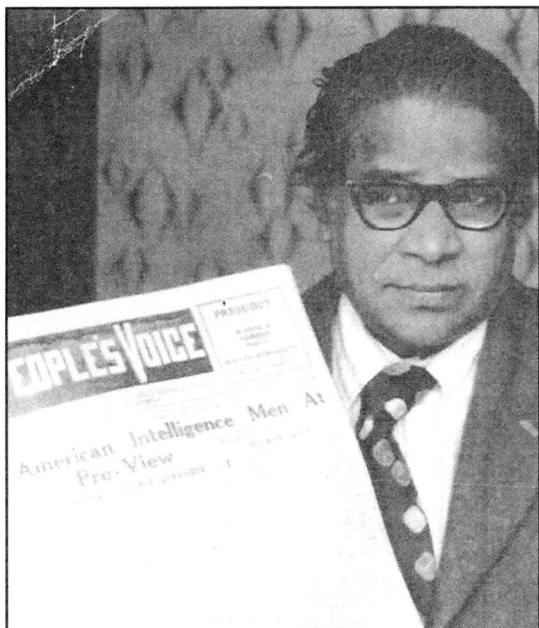

Right:
As a Journalist, Vaikuntha Vasan displaying his Tabloid; when he was the Editor and Publisher of *People's Voice.*

Below:
The Ceylon delegation arriving with sparkling jubilation in Beijing for the *Asian & Pacific Conference*(1952). Vaikuntha Vasan (3rd from left donning the socialist cap).

Above:
Vaikuntha Vasan-as vice-
chairman of the Economic
Commission, made an impact
with his address, to the
Beijing Peace Conference.
(See pages 98-102)
Right: the Peace Slogans in
the Conference Hall.

和平萬歲

ДА ЗДРАВСТВУЕТ МИР
ВО ВСЕМ МИРЕ !

LONG LIVE PEACE !

VIVA LA PAZ !

In dedicated atten-
tion at the Beijing
Conference(l-r):
Mrs. Vaikuntha
Vasan,
Shanmugathasan,
delegation leader
Rev.Narawila
Dhammaratna; and
Vaikuntha Vasan
(2nd row right).

Right: On the eve of the farewell, the delegation with Yo Dai Heng, the official interpreter/ host, and the socialist leader Philip Gunawardena (both in centre).

Below:
Mrs. Vaikuntha Vasan performing on the **Veena** during a reception to the Chinese Trade Union delegation. As a companion, secretary, proof reader and motivator- Maheswary was the driving force behind the success of this legendary Campaigner-lawyer.

Above:
The ever friendly Chinese hosts bidding farewell to the Ceylon delegation; waving with flowers and chanting peace.

Right:
In the USSR, the delegation visited the colossal **Moscow University**;with1,500 Professors and 11,000 students...graduating students were offered immediate jobs.

Left:
The delegation inside a textile factory in Georgia. Unemployment was Nil in the USSR.

Below:
On a tour of a tea plantation in Georgia.Collective Farms were a success in the USSR.

Left: Vaikuntha Vasans amidst the farmers at the headquarters of the Collective Farm of Natanabai, Georgia, USSR

Below: In the **Kremlin Museum** in Moscow with the horse carriages used by the Tsars of Russia.

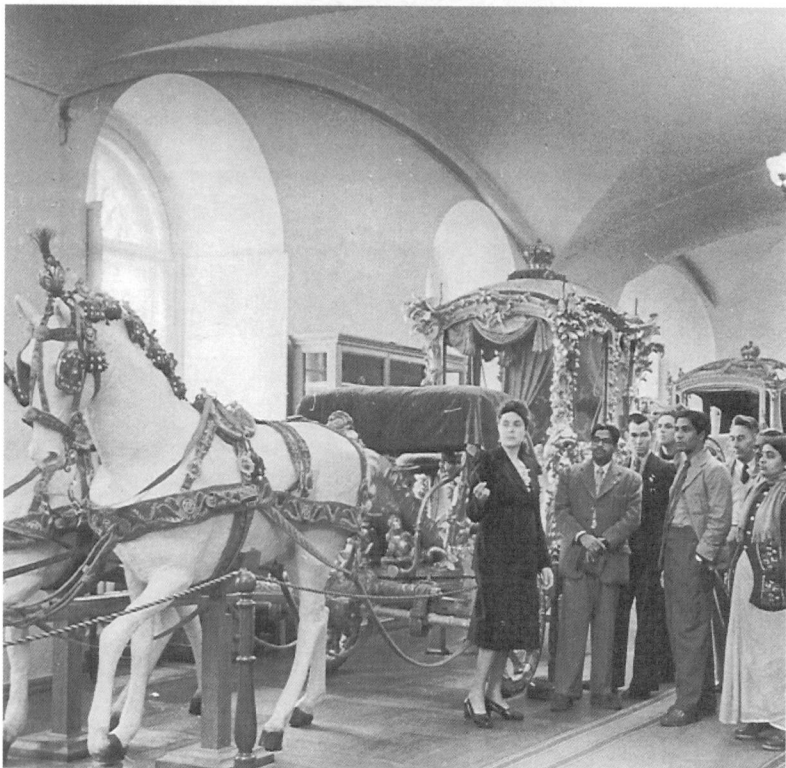

Chapter 5

Humanist at Heart and Socialist in Action

The Purpose of Life is a Life of Purpose
-Robert Byrne

Vaikuntha Vasan's life was filled with Purpose and his was a life of Purpose. Although he started his career as a clerk in the Ceylon Government Service, he had embraced a very active role in the Government Service Trade Union Movement from the very beginning. It was from the GCSU a well-known contraction for the Government Clerical Service Union, that Vaikuntha Vasan's ascent began.

To understand the personality such as Vaikuntha Vasan as he was, it is imperative to go back to his earlier days for a moment. He was a student of Jaffna College, of Vaddukoddai, in the Jaffna Peninsula; a College set up by the American missionaries to gain a foothold in the Intellectual heartland of Ceylon. There, as a student he raised the very purpose of Life. He asked this question at a religious class to a highly respected educationist of Jaffna- Mr. Handy Perinpanayagam: "No one knows

for certain what Life is all about. There have been many
Interpretations. And why should there be so many religions. It
simply baffles me"? "I don't know"! Replied the greatest educationist of Jaffna, "Even the greatest minds have failed to
answer". This was in 1937. He was 17. And there after
Vaikuntha Vasan went his own way to find the answer to the
question that was agitating at the back of his mind – the
Purpose of Life. Instead of becoming a wandering monk seeking for the answer – he evolved into a man of Karma – finding
the answer through selfless action. This selfless, but purposeful
action was what led Vaikuntha Vasan to get into full steam into
the Trade Union Movement of Ceylon.

But to become an action man of Karma, one of the key ingredi-
ents is courage; courage with conviction. This, the young
Vaikuntha Vasan exhibited at another occasion, at a major
Tamil political meeting in Colombo in 1944. He was 24. It was
a major political meeting that even moulded the political destiny of the Tamil Nation eventually to lead to an adverse course.
The founding day of the Tamil Congress political party by G.
G. Ponnambalam, who was later to become a key figure in
Tamil politics and also a minister in the independent Island
nation's cabinet. Vaikuntha Vasan made his way to the platform
of this inaugural meeting of the All-Ceylon Tamil Congress
held at the Saiva Mangayar Kazhagam (Hindu Ladies College),
at Wellawatte, Colombo. There he called upon the leader of the
new party, G. G. Ponnambalam: Not to proceed with the formation of a purely Tamil Organisation; but instead to form an
All-Island Minorities Congress to include all the minorities in
Ceylon. It fell on deaf ears of the stubborn leader. If only G. G
Ponnambalam listened to Vailkuntha Vasan, the disaster of the
past five decades could have been clearly averted well in
advance. But alas, instead, the Cambridge trained Tamil

Congress leader, later went on and played the fascist card of 50:50 – equal representation for Tamils and Sinhalese in the Legislative; and all mayhem was let loose from thereon - with worse retaliation to follow from Sinhala fascism! What a visionary was Vaikuntha Vasan; but also a man of conviction and courage; and above all a humanly socialist at heart. For he did not see a difference between a Tamil and a Sinhalese; For him all humanity is equal. And they are born equal.

Vaikuntha Vasan's background at birth and upbringing had a lot to do with his humanism and socialism. He was born to traditional middle class Hindu parents: Krishna Pillai and Lakshmi Ammal. Krishna Pillai hailed from Alaveddy, one of the largest villages in the Jaffna Peninsula. Alaveddy has produced its own share of leading administrators and professionals for Sri Lanka. Krishna Pillai, who was a young clerical officer in Malaya, returned abruptly back to Ceylon following the death of his parents. He later wandered seeking to find Truth, undertaking pilgrimages to numerous holy shrines in India. He sought audiences with and attended spiritual lectures given by holy men in India. On returning back to his village in Ceylon, his relatives promptly arranged his marriage to Lakshmi Ammal. On the very first day of the marriage Krishna Pillai gave a lengthy sermon to the wedding guests... It was on the *Purpose of Life* itself!

Lakshmi Ammal, his mother, emanates from Karainagar – where Vaikuntha Vasan was born on 15th April 1920. Karainagar is an Island northwest of the Jaffna Peninsula. Each region and island in the Jaffna Peninsula, curiously has its own salient features and quality of people. Perhaps to do with the variety of the soil, but more to do with the lineages over many centuries that took root in different parts of the Peninsula. Karainagar had a striking strain of orthodoxy with a high percentage of healthy vegetarians, who were devout Shaivites, with close links to nearby Vedaranniyam and Chidambaram , across the Palk Strait, in Tamil Nadu. The Karainagar island has also produced many financially prudent businessmen. Vaikuntha Vasan coming from this maternal lineage, had also acquired the healthy life-style and financial prudence of Karainagar. And added to it the administrative professionalism of Alaveddy.

Vaikuntha Vasan's educational career as a child was in his maternal Karainagar; later moving onto his paternal village of Alaveddy, where he continued at the Alaveddy Elementary Boys' School (which later was renamed Arunodaya College), and completed his Junior School Certificate in 1938. It is from here he moved onto Jaffna College at Vaddukoddai to pursue his studies for London Matriculation examinations. Jaffna College was established as mentioned earlier by the American Christian Missionaries. This Institution was the biggest educational venture by the Americans in the sub-continent, including Ceylon. Boasting the best school library in Asia, Vaikuntha Vasan eagerly created his own niche in this Institution to nourish his intellectual hunger.

Every day in the morning Vaikuntha Vasan could be seen scrambling into the elite library of Jaffna College, seated there and gathering the worldly knowledge that the Americans were generously providing with. He even ignored the customary daily assembly and the mass. For he affirmed to himself:" I have come here to study; not to attend Christian mass!" For he could not see the logic behind the imposition of oneself into a daily Christian mass.

It was not long before, one day, young Vaikuntha Vasan was brought to task. Jaffna College had its own salients. The Librarians of this Institution were notoriously well known for being strict task masters maintaining pin drop silence and order. Tipped off by the Librarian, Vaikuntha Vasan was taken to task by the supremo of that College – Mr. Bignell. Vaikuntha Vasan was immersed in his studies on that morning, when suddenly he felt a hand strongly pressing his shoulder. "What the hell are you doing here"? thundered, the red faced principal, Mr. Bignell. "You should be at the Assembly should'nt you"? he asserted.   And he led the young man gently away from the library to the Assembly platform.

"I was only a youngster at that time; otherwise I would have defied the compulsory induction into the masses" regretted Vaikuntha Vasan, when asked about his feelings of that incident: and he continued "We went there to study not to attend ritual masses"!   Inherently confident and proud of his ancestral Tamil Shaivaite philosophy and culture of many thousands of years, Vaikuntha Vasan resisted the colonial. "Brain Programming" through Christianity, that was to eventually drive the Jaffna society into conflicting odds with the rest of the Indian sub-continental masses, including the Sinhalese.

It is also interesting to note that the vast Jaffna College campus – somewhat an Oxbridge of Ceylon, also became the citadel of anti-communism and pro-Federal Party, the Party   founded by SJV Chelvanayagam and his associates to demand a   Federal State for the Tamils, within Ceylon. With the intellectual surge around the Jaffna College campus, there also grew a socialist thinking, which also influenced Vaikuntha Vasan. But the budding communism was countered with active sponsorship of

Tamil nationalism. The role played by Jaffna College authorities, standing at the intersection of a vital point of the peninsula, is still shrouded in mystery. Many even suspected that Jaffna College willingly acted as a cover for American CIA operations. These are of course conjectures; any evidence if at all would have been long extinguished through the shredding machines.

Having qualified in the London Matriculation examinations in 1938, Vaikuntha Vasan sat for the Ceylon Clerical Service examinations to enter the government service. Having passed, as always with merit, he was placed in the Auditor-General's Department, as was the practice, where the first ten selected go to work for. Here too, Vaikuntha Vasan did not spare from enacting a sensational act.

At the annual general meeting of the Auditor-General's Staff Association, the then acting Auditor-General was addressing the gathering. On announcing his assumption of the post as the new acting Auditor-General, the new incumbent said: "I am sure you all realise that, you are all expected to be 99% accurate in your audit work". Then when the question time came, a young man suddenly arose from the far end of the 200 members packed hall, and said: Sir, you are addressing the officers of the Auditor-General's Department. We are therefore expected to be 100% accurate; how can you, sir, say that we are expected to be 99% accurate? There was a spontaneous accolade that greeted Vasan: "Sir, please acknowledge your mistake for what you said is wrong"demanded the young officer. Apology promptly followed the request of this rebellious intellect.

The Trade Union Leader

Vaikuntha Vasan's induction into the GCSU (Government Clerical Service Union) was a boon not merely for the Trade Union Movement of Ceylon; but even for the progress of Socialism that later swept into power a progressive coalition. It was also remarkable that for a person who joined as an ordinary clerk to have become the General-Secretary of a vital Trade Union within a few years. And that too to be elected unanimously for the services rendered.

The GCSU, it is worthy to mention was the most powerful Trade Union with a membership of 13,000 clerical servants, that administered the government machinery itself. And it was built with the blood, tears and sweat of a loyal and dedicated membership. Vaikuntha Vasan was elected the General Secretary of the GCSU in 1948 and also edited the Union Journal: Red Tape. But even before that he organised the All-Island Middle Class and Public Service Trade Unions in 1947 and remained its Joint-Secretary for three years.

The GCSU was set up in 1920 to serve the needs of the government clerical service workers of the Island. The severe economic depression and rumblings of discontent at the end of the first world-war saw the rise of organised trade unionism in England. Following the foot steps of England and fearing the loss of economic status and privileges, the idea was brought forth, in the Ceylon Clerical Service to set up a central body for the General Clerical Service. And so in 1920, the GCSU was inaugurated. But the organisation was never registered as a trade union, as it was felt by the clerical workers that trade unions were only meant for manual workers! And as such no active role was played by this body until 1947. The Organisation became notoriously powerful only with the General Strike of 1947. The GCSU urged the public servants to revolt against the Government in a bid to secure full trade union rights and to obtain a decent living wage. It was a revolt against a right wing government. There was mass uprising among the worker force in Colombo. Police opened fire at a workers procession led by the socialist leaders Dr. N. M. Perera and Dr. Colvin R. de Silva – who became the leaders of the powerful leftist LSSP(Lanka Sama Samaja Party) and Pieter Keuneman and Dr. S.A. Wickremasinghe – the Communist Party leaders. Several were injured and a clerical officer Mr. V. Kandasamy became the first martyr of the labour movement of Ceylon. The imperial government was shaken and caved in to the militant demands of the GCSU. The GCSU, the first middle class trade union of the Island nation, is credited to have accelerated in its own way for the British to leave Ceylon.

Vaikuntha Vasan played a few key roles in the GCSU before and while his period of being the General Secretary of the GCSU. This had elevated the GCSU to a powerful position in the socio-political spectrum of the Island of Ceylon.

The GCSU had since its inception in 1920, was far from a trade union organisation. It was not even registered as a trade union. When in 1935 the Ceylon State Council passed the Trade Union Ordinance No.14 of 1935, it invited for trade unions such as the GCSU to register itself as a Trade Union. The GCSU ignored this Ordinance. When asked for explanation of this lapse, the then Secretary of the GCSU resenting that it was beneath its dignity to be called a trade union; replied to the Registrar of Trade Unions: "Clerks are not labourers and that trade unions were only for labourers." It was preposterous that only a few years later a massive agitation had to be mounted by the GCSU, to extract from the government the very same right that was earlier forced upon it but rejected. With the promise of full responsible self-government, and the Public Service becoming the responsibility of a locally elected minister, the GCSU decided to demand for Trade Union rights and Civil Liberties. As mentioned above the General Strike of 1947 brought victory to the GCSU. And after being elected to the Office of General Secretary; it was Vaikuntha Vasan, who expedited the registration of the GCSU as a Trade Union in December 1949. It was also one of the achievements in his capacity as the General Secretary of this Organisation.

One of the direct effects of the agitation for Trade Union rights was the invitation, following its Annual General Meeting in December 1946, of the leaders of the Marxist Movement in Ceylon to speak at union meetings. This alarmed the conservative President A. T. Murthy, who resigned from Office. The privately owned National Media sensing the dangers of socialism sweeping the Island, introduced the communal element by reporting in its columns that the GCSU was dominated by the minority Tamil community! But no non-Tamil in Colombo was forthcoming to contest for the now vacant post. There was at the same time, a momentum of massive agitation building up for trade union rights; with the launch of a Trade Union Week. Trade Union Week was organised to conduct classes for the public servants on instilling in them the spirit of trade unionism and political and civil liberties. There was also a "Declaration of Rights of Ceylon Public Servants" that had to be read in all meetings. The GCSU had also planned to wind up the Trade Union Week with a massive procession and meeting. All these

could not be manoeuvred upon without a President. Sensing
the dangers of the new scenario, Vaikuntha Vasan made his
astute move. He brought a no-confidence move against the
Council of Management, who showed no concern for the great
lapse of not having a President to lead.

A President had to be found soon to lead the GCSU; and it had
to be a non-Tamil, to overcome the communal card sown by
imperial agents. The Kandy provincial GCSU branch was led
then by a not so ambitious T. B. Ilangaratne, a local clerical servant. But it was also the Kandy branch of the GCSU, with T. B.
Ilangaratne as its President, that had fired its first salvo, by
appealing to the Ceylon State Council to support the demand
for Trade Union rights. Here again Vaikuntha Vasan made his
move swiftly. He persuaded the shy T. B. Ilangaratne to accept
the Presidency of the GCSU. Which he did; and Vaikuntha
Vasan followed suit by withdrawing his no-confidence motion.
The GCSU had now a leader – T.B. Ilangaratne - acceptable by
all. The GCSU became a formidable force thereafter culminating in the General Strike of 1947. It is noteworthy that when the
socialist forces took power in 1956 T. B. Ilangaratne became a
cabinet minister, holding the post of Trade and Commerce.

The third contribution befitting Vaikuntha Vasan in the trade
union movement was his role as the editor of the Red Tape - the
official organ of the GCSU. The Red Tape was launched by the
GCSU, in December 1941, copying the name of the journal
then published by its counterpart- the Civil Service Clerical
Association of England. His bold and brave editorials embarrassed the right wing government of independent Ceylon.
Vaikuntha Vasan was dismissed from government service in
August 1950, for writing in the Red Tape of accusing the gover-

nment as responsible for the killing of the trade union martyr V. Kandasamy back in 1947. The Government acting under the Ceylon Administrative Regulations (AR) cited that Vaikuntha Vasan had breached section 208B; whereby there was a specific ban on any political activity by all government servants. As a consequence he had to forfeit his positions in the GCSU as well. A man of boldness and courage, and a humanist at heart, Vaikuntha Vasan proved decisively to be a Socialist in Action!

Having lost his government job and powerful positions in the GCSU; he was not let down by his Purpose in Life; and was not let down by his comrades in action either. For the comrades promptly reinstated him in the government service at a later time, when the socialist forces gained political power in 1956; and also assisted him, while he was out of a job, to get in with the next stage of his action- the launch of the *People's Voice.*

Chapter 6

People's Voice
The Independent
Newsweekly

The voice of the people is the voice of God
Vox populi, vox dei
– Alcuin, Epistle to Charlemagne

The only thing that is greater than the power of the mind is the courage of the heart. With the most intense courage Vaikuntha Vasan embarked on his journalistic career, supported by a plethora of leading personalities and comrades in action. And with a bang the People's Voice was launched on 19th January 1951; filling the news stalls and the Trade Union offices – throughout the length and breadth of the Island. The first Issue was dedicated with a front page of the broadsheet carrying a photograph of the fellow comrade and martyr V. Kandasamy, who succumbed to police firing at the workers' procession during the general strike of 1947.

Vaikuntha Vasan's potential, as a great journalist, was revealed throughout the three years of the publication of this independ -

ent weekly. The People's Voice acquired importance in filling a void in the post independent era, barely three years within the British left Ceylon. With the national press in the hands of vested private interests, People's Voice assumed a key role in shaping the socialist forces of the Island.

In the first Issue of the weekly, Vaikuntha Vasan emphasised the need for an independent English Newspaper that will neither slavishly ditto the fiats of the Government nor mechanically echo the slogans of its opponents. Captioned: "Ourselves", Vaikuntha Vasan penned: We have come forward to meet the need… borne out by the gathering momentum of a three month campaign which claims its strength not from a few thousand–rupee donations but from thousands of people who have contributed only their subscriptions to make possible the emergence of their voice on a national scale. Assured, therefore, of this inexhaustible popular source…we shall go to the same source for our news, confident in the belief that truth is where life is and life is where people are. He called upon the readers to express the monsoonal force of public opinion and make the paper their own in a more real and lasting sense.

Interestingly the front page headline news of the very first Issue was; "American Intelligence Men At Pre-View": A whole exposure of how the new right wing Mayor of Colombo V. Sellamuthu, the Inspector General of Police Sir Richard Aluvihare, and the Superintendent of the Police CID branch Mr. Koelmeyer, tried their utmost to sabotage the Soviet Film Festival in Colombo. The People's Voice reported:

From the "Daily News" to the American Embassy, all reactionaries sat up and took notice and tried their utmost to sabotage it. The new mayor obligingly played his part. Sir John Kotelawela, propaganda chief of the ruling United National Party (UNP) came next to the Saphire Theatre. But wait. Then come the real masters of the UNP and Ceylon – a high-ranking official of the American Embassy, American Naval Intelligence Officers in uniform and an official of the British Embassy. Why had these representatives of foreign powers come to a pre-view, which is entirely an internal matter? Had they come to decide for the UNP Mayor what films were fit to be passed?

Sir John Kotelawela, in his usual manner, threw his weight about the place, shouted at everybody, and demanded to know who was organising the festival and who was getting the money etc. When told by the organisers that similar festivals had been organised in Bombay and Calcutta and several leading figures in Indian public life had associated themselves with the festival, Sir John shouted; "I don't care what happens in India. We are the government here and I will not allow this sort of thing." ... Eventually they saw several reels of several films and could find nothing objectionable. Sir John sneaked out half way, calling out to the Mayor: "Do as I told you". The Mayor and his American advisers stayed on. But the films were of such a high standard and so un-objectionable that these gentlemen could not find any reason for stopping them... People's Voice goes further into its investigative reporting:

But this is not the only instance of interference by the American Embassy in connection with this film festival. We are in a position to reveal that the American Embassy sent a letter to the head of a Colombo establishment drawing his attention to the fact that an employee of his was taking an active part in organising the Soviet Film Festival. Could interference in internal affairs by a foreign government go further? We thought we were independent. So reported the People's Voice.

The People's Voice was boldly truthful in its news reporting week after week and stuck to the declared objectives of Truth is where Life is. Looking back in perspective, historians could easily retrace the scenarios that led to the political turmoil that descended on newly independent nations through foreign interferences. The wealthy Sir John Kotelawela, it should be noted eventually became the Prime Minister of Ceylon, stupefied the economy, muddled the Language Issue-resulting eventually in the communal riots, lost the elections and took refuge in the Garden County of Kent, in England. He thereafter lived a flamboyant – and romantic life with all the comforts provided for. The masses of his native Sri Lanka, both the Singhalese and the Tamils, descended into a miserable lot with strife, poverty and vagrancy.

The People's Voice was famous among other things for witty cartoons. Vaikuntha Vasan had recruited and groomed the most talented young artist – Siva Gnana Sundaram, a draughtsman from the Public Works Department, to give cartoon presentation to the contemporary news. Siva Gnana Sundaram had his training in Art in Bombay. Every week Vaikuntha Vasan ensured the Paper had the most appealing and witty cartoons. They are superb even to today's standards. Siva Gnana Sundaram became famous through the People's Voice, and later launched his own cartoon – humour magazine **Siriththiran** –which became a household Journal in the Tamil homeland.

The People's Voice was not merely a newspaper. There were in depth coverage in the fields of art and science. The very first Issue carried a lengthy article from a famous Indian scientist

Prof. D.D. Kosambi - on the benefits of Atomic Power to
Mankind. A subsequent issue even had an informed report trac-
ing as to who really owned the U.S. atom bombs. Articles on
economics enlightened the readers with emphasis on cost of living crisis and inflation. Reportage on international affairs
abounded the weekly, educating the readers country by country.
Letters to the Editor had full bags. People's Voice became the
listening post for complaints and suggestions on hospital services, bus services, library services etc.

Vaikuntha Vasan also had interviewed many personalities in his
span as the editor of People's Voice. Among them were:
S.W.R.D. Bandaranaike (the first socialist Prime Minister),
R.K. Karanjia (Editor of the popular socialist weekly from
Bombay – BLITZ), N.S. Krishnan (Comedy actor and
reformer) and many political and judicial services personalities.

There were interesting short articles on Life Issues; and snip-
pets of humour, humorous poems, quotations etc. The film
reviews were of a highly critique form with verdicts. There
were advertisements; but that took only smaller space of the
whole Paper. Vaikuntha Vasan had care given to every detail
and section; which gave a unique power to the whole paper. For
a full six months, due to popular demand, the paper even
became a bi-weekly rolling out of the press every Wednesday
and Saturday. Vaikuntha Vasan had involved his family in the
Press. His dutiful wife Maheswary, of whom more in a later
chapter, assisted in every stage and held the title of Manager of
the People's Voice. His father Krishna Pillai was the Manager
of the People's Press, which rolled out the paper - on time week
after week. The People's Voice was the only
English opposition paper and proclaimed: *To Speak for you; To*

Fight for you; and To Win for you.

But the reactionary forces of the newly independent Ceylon were mightier than the progressive forces. They sat back and took note of the publication as a threat to their vested interests. They therefore saw to it that the People's Voice did not continue for long. When asked what made him to wind up the Press; Vaikuntha Vasan bluntly stated that the People's Voice was never shut down; "We sold the Press to Mrs. Theja Gunawardena another socialist-Ceylonese Journalist." Theja and comrades thereafter used the Printing Press to roll out publications under different titles and continued the work that Vaikuntha Vasan began.

The thrilling adventures of publishing the People's Voice depicted guerrilla warfare in journalism! Vaikuntha Vasan having bought the printing machine from India, set up his Press in First Division, Maradana, Colombo. It was within a hotel complex. The Police started their harassment from day one. They accused the Press as a Communist outfit. The landlords gave notice to quit. They then moved to Rajagiriya, east of Colombo city. Vaikuntha Vasans thereafter moved lock stock and barrel to Angulana; and then from there to Ratmalana near the airport and finally to Kelaniya, north of Colombo.

The People's Voice was published with a great deal of support from clerical officers in government service. As such inside sources often tipped off the Vaikuntha Vasans even before the Police raided the premises. There were news and contributions that were forthcoming under pseudo names from government servants; Vaikuntha Vasans' first task therefore was to hide or destroy the identities of the contributors in advance. It was scorched earth warfare in journalism.

The right wing government did not spare a single strategy to bring the Press down on its knees. They pressurised the advertisers to withdraw advertising. That was the final straw. Being dried up of funds, Vaikuntha Vasan decided to call it off. But, within the three years, they had achieved what even the mega right wing press could not. It is an undisputed fact that the socialist landscape of today's Sri Lanka owes a lot to Vaikuntha Vasan.

N. S. Krishnan, one of the greatest south Indian comedy actors cum intellectual of the mid 20th century, said this of the People's Voice in his appreciative message: ***Were it left for me to decide whether we should have a Government without Newspapers or Newspapers without a Government - I should not hesitate a moment to prefer the latter.*** He wished that the People's Voice continued to be the Chosen Guardian of Freedom, the Strong sword-arm of Justice and the Bright Sunbeam of Truth. The People's Voice had praises coming in from many leaders and intellects. S.W.R.D. Bandaranaike, the leader of the Sri Lanka Freedom Party, who later became Prime Minister, had to depend on the People's Voice for the progress in his political career, and praised: ***The People's Voice by its courageous and independent attitude had performed a great service to the people.*** Vaikuntha Vasan crowned his journalistic career with such praise and recognition, making the Voice of the People equal to the Voice of God.

Chapter 7

Three Months in China and Soviet Union

We shall find peace.
We shall hear the angels,
We shall see the sky
Sparkling with diamonds.
- Anton Chekhov

At a most momentous period of time in world history; in a post World War II era, with the Korean conflict heightening the cold war, Vaikuntha Vasan began his three months' journey to China, the Soviet Union and Austria, to take part in international peace conferences.   Having been elected the Joint Secretary of the Ceylon Preparatory Committee for the Asian and Pacific Peace Conference, he was fittingly chosen to be a delegate to the peace conferences held in Beijing, China-October 1952 and in Vienna, Austria-December 1952. There were ten personalities of prominence in the team, led by a socialist Buddhist religious leader Rev. Narawila Dhammaratna.

For Vaikuntha Vasan this was a great experience and an exposure to life in two great socialist countries; and to two grand
peace conferences, summoned to stave off another world war.
These experiences have been suitably captured by him in his
Book: Three Months in New China & Soviet Union. A masterpiece in travel writing, that dwarfs Bill Bryson's travelogues, in
its quality of human understanding and purpose of life. At a
time when there was unabated war mongering by imperialist
forces, Vaikuntha Vasan was able to see in person and report the
yearning for peace and the vast progress made by the people of
China and the USSR.

In Canton, South China the starting point of his tour, he saw
enthusiastic young pioneers of the Canton Peace Committee
according a rousing welcome with lovely bouquets of flowers
amidst thunderous chanting of Hoping Wangsuwe (Long Live
Peace). An instance of hospitality where the girl in a host house
enthusiastically prepared tea for the delegates, danced with joy,
hugged, kissed, and greeted with the slogan: Long Live the
Friendship between the Peoples of Ceylon and China; and Long
Live World Peace! Even as they travelled by train through
China hundreds of young boys and girls greeted the delegates
with flowers and chanting of Hoping Wangsuwe.

The peace delegates were elated with excitement when on the
eve of the Chinese National Day; they were invited along with
foreign diplomats and model workers for a grand banquet given
by Chairman Mao Tse-tung. Flanked by the Chinese Prime
Minister Chou En-lai and Chu Teh, the Commander-in-Chief,
Chairman Mao proposed a toast to the 2,000 guests, amidst
deafening applause and cheers. Vaikuntha Vasan in his youthful
curiosity managed to leave his table and go near Mao to get a
glimpse of him. He was greatly inspired and overjoyed on see-
ing Mao. When after Chou En-lai came to their table and pro-

posed a toast, Vaikuntha Vasan and another comrade followed him from table to table listening to his messages and toasts. The whole gathering felt highly honoured; Vaikuntha Vasan and his delegation returned to their hotels singing happily.

Vaikuntha Vasan recalls to memory the Chinese National Day celebrations in Tein An Men (The Gate of Heavenly Peace) Square in the heart of Beijing. Following the parade of the soldiers, there was an impressive march past by hundreds of thousands of Chinese workers. Tens of thousands of little boys and girls came next, bursting with joy, chanting Long Live Peace, as they passed Chairman Mao, members of the government, and the delegates. "One of the greatest sights I have ever seen in my life" pronounced Vaikuntha Vasan. The little children in their white uniforms with white doves in their hands were so sweet and lovely that they looked like angels. They let the doves fly into the air and thousands of white doves were in the sky presenting a beautiful sight, sparkling like diamonds.

The Ceylonese delegation entered China, by train from Hong Kong. Vaikuntha Vasan contrasts the sights of Hong Kong to that of in Mainland China. He compares the facial expressions of the soldiers of the Chinese People's Liberation Army (PLA) to the pitiable sights of the British soldiers he saw on the Hong Kong side of the border. He was stressed to see hundreds of young British soldiers marching with dejected faces, without any enthusiasm, like men being taken to the gallows. The PLA on the other hand had earned a good name among the people for their exemplary behaviour and patriotism. They were surcharged with emotion and had a feeling of comradeship; and were regarded by the Chinese people as the apple of their eyes. Similarly he describes the degradation of Hong Kong, where he saw Chinese girls, lips blood red with lipstick and dishevelled hair, anxiously waiting to be picked up. In Mainland China he could not see such sights; and he says it is incredible that both belonged to the same Chinese Nation. In the streets of Hong Kong he said he was followed by a number of beggars. But he did not see a single beggar anywhere in China.

Vaikuntha Vasan in his pro-active posture made friends wherever he went. One was Walter Illsley, an American engineer resident in China. He narrated the economic life in China before and after the revolution. During the pre-revolution period, one day, Walter had sat down in a hotel for a meal. While he was eating the waiter came along and told him that the prices had been doubled. And when he finished his meals and went to pay the bill, he had to pay three times the original price that was shown in the menu. That was how the spiralling inflation affected the Kuomintang (Guomindang-the regime led by the Chinese rightwing nationalist President Chiang Kai-shek) currency. But Walter praised the conditions under the communist regime and expressed his conviction that no power on earth, no American atom bomb would be able to destroy the new spirit of the Chinese people. Walter Illsley, a US citizen himself, and an American delegate to the Peace Conference, had this to say: If only the common people of the United States knew the truth about the Korean war, they would never have tolerated the present American policy. What is happening in America is that the reactionary Government with its stupendous network of radio, television and press, is able to confuse and mislead the common people. The irony is that brainwashing through the media power is still there in the USA and nothing has changed significantly even after a period of fifty years.

The historic Peace Conference of the Asian and Pacific regions was held in Beijing from October 2nd to October 13th, 1952 with 400 delegates from 37 countries, representing 1,600 million people.

Soong Ching-ling, wife of the Chinese revolutionary leader Sun Yut-sen (1867-1925) declared open the Peace Conference amidst thunderous applause, and said: "We must mobilise the people to demand that all present wars cease and be settled peacefully, through sincere negotiations... that all weapons of mass destruction be abolished and outlawed and that all barriers to trade and cultural exchange be broken down...and we must mobilise the people to strive for the moral conditions which make for peaceful co-existence."

Ivor Montagu, Secretary of the World Peace Council, made one of the most powerful and moving speeches. He enumerated the crimes against humanity committed by the British colonialists in Malaya and thundered: "I take this forum to declare, the following deeds in Malaya: destruction of crops, use of chemicals in warfare, razing of village property, collective punishment, torture of prisoners, and defilement of the dead. Every one of these are crimes against humanity...based not on a disputed complaint but is authenticated by admission, even boasts, of the authorities responsible for committing them..."

Meanwhile, Dr. Chen Wen-kuei, well known bacteriologist of China, related what he had personally witnessed and investigated in regard to the use of bacteriological weapons in Korea, and North East China by the US armed forces.Pandit C.N.Malaviya, the Indian Parliamentarian, denounced the inhuman actrocities committed by the invaders in Korea, Vietnam and Malaya. Mrs. Manjusree Chattopadhyayah, the Indian delegate described the suffering and death brought to India's women and children by war, and the economic chaos caused by war preparations; and urged women to defend peace. Ceylon Parliamentarian Edmund Samarakkody emphasised the direct connection between wars and imperialism; and urged for the widest application of the united front method.

Important issues were then discussed, researched and resolved at the Conference. Delegates were divided into eight commissions with freedom to join any commission they liked. The commissions were beautifully organised; lasting ten days, with open discussions, cordiality and unanimous decisions. Then major resolutions were put forth as follows: 1. An all-in solution to the Japanese question and the curbing of Japanese militarism. 2. Ending of the Korean War. 3. The safeguarding of the national independence of peoples of all countries.   4. The issue of economic development. 5. Cultural exchange between nations.   6. Safeguarding women's rights. 7. Programme for child welfare. 8. Five-Power Peace Pact (between USA, USSR, UK, France and China). And 9. Establishment of a Peace Liaison Committee of the Asian and Pacific regions.

As the vice-chairman of the Economic Commission, and on behalf of the Ceylon delegation, Vaikuntha Vasan had the unique honour of speaking at the conference. He was highly elated when at the end of his twenty minutes speech the Chinese leaders including Madame Sun Yat-sen congratulated him. He submitted an enlightening report on the question of economic relations. It was a very pertinent report which only revealed Vaikuntha Vasan's masterly grasp of the then complicated theatre of international economics.

He began his address thus: Mr. Chairman, fellow delegates and friends! On behalf of the peace-loving people of Ceylon, I greet this historic conference! Before I submit my report I wish to state that after the comprehensive reports on the subject placed before you by the previous speakers this morning, it would be unnecessary for me to go into any of the general problems concerning this subject. I shall therefore confine myself only to a few aspects, which are of special significance to Ceylon.

One of the direct and immediate results of war preparations and the "cold war" has been the dislocation of normal trade relations between countries of the world. It is an admitted fact that the establishment of mutually advantageous trade relations between countries helps in the preservation of peace.

The heightening of war tension in the world today has resulted in the division of the world into blocs of countries. Trade relations between these blocs have diminished to such an extent as to cause disastrous results in the economies of some of these countries. This policy of a trade embargo against those countries that refuse to toe her line has been pursued by the Government of the USA in furtherance of her aggressive aims. Not only has the USA herself refused to trade with those countries whose ideology and political structure do not conform to her liking, but she has also used her dominant economic position following the last war to force those countries, whose economies have been destroyed by war as well as by years of colonial exploitation and who, therefore, stood in need of economic assistance by the more advanced countries, to desist from trading with those same countries on pain of losing American economic aid.

Vaikuntha Vasan went on further to illustrate the case of what was happening to his own country. The economic dependency of having to export the precious raw materials to USA-UK, merely to obtain in return the basic consumer products from these countries, itself has been disastrously affected, due to the increased war preparations by both USA-UK. They are not in a position to supply our essential import needs, as also the capital equipment for the much publicised development projects. Further more, the prices they paid for our primary export products kept falling compared to the prices we paid for the goods they sent us.

He cited the issue of rubber exports to the USA: The USA, he said, used her monopoly power as the largest buyer of rubber to force down the price and as such the revenue obtained through the export of rubber from Ceylon fell from Rupees 29.4million in December 1950 to Rupees 2.5million in September 1951. This had affected the Island nation's economy adversely as its national income depended mainly on the export of the three main commodities of tea, rubber and coconut. This had also resulted in wage cuts, retrenchment, closures, mass unemployment and cuts in social services.

But, he said, the problem is not without its solution. Today there are alternative markets for our export commodities. But because of the "Cold war" we are prevented from trading with countries like the Soviet Union and New China, which want to buy our goods and sell us what we need. The American government has threatened to stop all forms of economic help if Ceylon trades with the USSR or New China, he said. He quoted how the Chinese procurement of rubber in large scale in the previous year had helped to stave off the price of rubber falling to disastrous levels.

Ceylon was also dependent on imports for two-thirds of its food requirements. As USA had bought up the rice from rice exporters in lieu of dollar payments, there was shortage of rice in the international market. In spite of American pressure, the Ceylon government has now sent a trade mission to Beijing to procure rice from China, which it has in plenty. What could be more natural and mutually advantageous than that we exchange rubber for rice with China? He said in his report.

Vaikuntha Vasan emphasised the role of industrialisation of undeveloped countries and said in his report that the Anglo-American bloc of countries had refused to supply capital equipment; the reason, he said, was that these countries wanted to keep the raw materials producing countries as their dumping ground for their consumer goods.

The Imperialists, he said, have of course, produced high-sounding plans like the 'Colombo Plan'. But even a mere cursory examination of these plans revealed their true nature. This plan was based on the expectation that America was not interested in any such financial injection. Even the 'Point Four Aid' which was never a serious proposition, was not forthcoming. Under the Colombo Plan, he said: all we can rely upon from the point of view of finance is the hope that the British Government will unfreeze those parts of our sterling balances which are legitimately due to us and return our money to us in the form of a loan. That is the Colombo Plan. The Colombo Plan is nothing more than the British Government lending us part of our money for our development. Our sterling balances were built up in England during the war and part of them are frozen in Number 2 Account. Now they are being released in driblets from No. 2 Account to No 1 Account - on which we are now drawing. That is the sum total of the bankrupt Colombo Plan.

It must also be noted, he said, that all the schemes under the Colombo Plan are such as would not change the dependent sta tus of our economy. All the schemes relate to improvement in transport and agriculture. None of them allow for the industrial development of our country. Even the International Bank Mission report has advised against all forms of industrial development and even large-scale agricultural schemes.

The right wing Ceylon government has been saying that there was difficulty in obtaining capital equipment for development. It was also part of the imperialist policy of keeping colonial countries dependent on their countries. Vaikuntha Vasan said: But we know that in the ECAFE Conference held in Rangoon, the Soviet delegate offered to supply machinery as well as other goods that are required. But such proposals are not taken advantage of by our Government because of American pressure and their embargo on trade with one half of the world. It is quite clear that only the full and free exchange of economic and trade relations between countries on a mutually advantageous relationship can, not only lessen the danger of war, but also lead to the development of the more backward countries - he concluded.

Vaikuntha Vasan saw in China and the USSR, that the workers, in whatever job or profession, commanded the highest respect and affection. He cites examples in his travelogue on the excellent conditions of the workers. In one occasion the hosts in a hotel in Canton feted the delegation. After dinner, while they were chatting to their hosts, a fellow delegate quietly drew the attention of Vaikuntha Vasan to the cushioned settee nearby and their occupants. He was so pleasantly surprised to recognise them as the waiters who had only been serving them dinner just a while ago. Once their job was over they were quietly resting as equals to any other fellow citizen.

Vaikuntha Vasan had visited a village in China and saw how the landless peasants were all liberated from ruthless landlords; and now having their own lands to work on. They all thanked the PLA and Chairman Mao for their economic freedom. The land had been redistributed equitably to all the peasants and there was success and collective productivity in that village. They also visited a village school. The system of education in the school was based on the five precepts of: *1. Love of country 2. Love of labour 3. Love of science 4. Love of public property and 5. Love of the people.*

Vaikuntha Vasan also visited the Bacteriological Warfare Exhibition in Beijing, where he saw concrete evidence and recorded confessions of American germ warfare. There he saw the actual bacteriological shells that had been dropped in Korea and North East China by the US armed forces. The delegation saw a vivid documentary film depicting the investigations carried out by the International Scientific Commission composed of eminent world scientists. "...Untune that string, And, hark, what discord follows!" said William Shakespeare (Troilus and Cressida). The imperialist forces did exactly this, by unleashing the germ warfare five decades ago. That has now become the ultimate weapon of bio-terrorism and is threatening to spread terrible discord throughout the world.

Vaikuntha Vasan and the Ceylonese delegation visited Universities, Factories, Housing Schemes, Kindergartens, Palaces of Culture, Workers Clubs, Libraries, Exhibitions, Co-operative Stores, Sanatoriums and a Buddhist Temple in their tour of Beijing, Tienstin, Shanghai and Hiang Chow.

Education in China was free throughout all levels and it was closely connected to China's vast scientific, industrial, agricultural, health and house building programmes to improve the living standards of the people. Chinese language is the medium of instruction. They visited the Beijing University (est: 1898) with more than 5,000 students; and where Chairman Mao had worked as a Librarian in 1918-1919. This is where Mao came in contact with Prof. Li Ta-chao, the pioneer who introduced Marxism into China. Vaikuntha Vasan was also shown the room where Prof. Li Ta-chao worked till 1927 and was assassinated along with 19 other student revolutionary leaders by the Kuomintang regime.

Housing development in China was at its supreme mode. They were constructed with speed; spacious, artistic and hygienic, and all amenities such as palace of culture, kindergarten, primary school, hospital, co-operative store, park, cinema house etc. provided. The rental was never more than 5% to 7% of the income of the family, compared to the West, where the rentals or it's another version called - mortgage, is an average of 50% to 70% of the income.

Vaikuntha Vasan observed that productivity in China was at a very high standard. China was producing all the electrical and mechanical goods including machine tools not only in huge quantities but also in high quality – thanks to the economic blockade of the USA. "This was because of the fact that the Chinese workers were putting their heart and soul into their work. Only in a country where they feel that they have a say in the government would workers work like this", said Vaikuntha Vasan. Vaikuntha Vasan was also invited to deliver a speech over the Radio Peking (Beijing) on the penultimate day of his stay in China. He said in his talk:

I have been in China for a month and a half, visiting places and studying the country. I have seen only one fly, no beggar, and no dejected face. And let us remember that three years ago no one could have counted the number of flies, beggars and the dejected faces. What has happened? A miracle you think. No. It is only this. The great Chinese people have discovered their own soul. They have risen as one man to the call of their beloved leader Mao Tse-tung.

The Chinese people desire peace. And they breathe peace. Said Vaikuntha Vasan. And the greatest guarantee to world peace lies in the ever-increasing ties of genuine friendship and mutual cooperation between China, Soviet Union, and the New Democracies, he said.

One Month In The Soviet Union

The peace delegation left China after thanking their hosts from the bottom of their hearts, for the great hospitality they had offered to them during their stay in China. It was a sad farewell at Beijing airport, but one that had elated immensely the hearts and souls of the delegates. After a brief reception by the Mongolian Peace committee at Ulan Bator, the capital of Mongolia, where Vaikuntha Vasan saw snow fall for the first time; the delegation reached the Soviet Union. The Ceylon peace delegation was visiting the Soviet Union at the invitation of the Central Council of the Trade Unions of the USSR.

Their first stop in the Soviet Union was Irkutsk, the Siberian town, which was under heavy snowfall at that time. Vaikuntha Vasan's first impression of the Soviet people was that they were all very healthy and sturdy. And had smiling faces with friend-ly looks. After Irkutsk, the delegation visited Novosibirsk,

Omsk, Sverdlovsk and finally they reached Moscow on November 6th. Vaikuntha Vasan could not forget the kindness and friendship shown by the Soviet people, especially the waitresses who served food, even though they could not communicate in a common language.

The first item on the Soviet itinerary was the great parade at Moscow's Red Square, on November 7th, where over half a million people participated. The army, navy, air force units and women's, youth and student organisations marched past in a tumultuous procession to celebrate the anniversary of their greatest day commemorating the October Revolution. There were flowers, banners, flags, placards, peace symbols; and pictures of Lenin, Stalin, Marx, Engels, Mao Tse-tung and Togliatti. Vaikuntha Vasan was surprised to see hundreds of thousands people immersing with joy, fervour, patriotism and enthusiasm when they saw Stalin and other leaders. He questioned the validity of the false propaganda unleashed in the non-communist world, of dictatorship and fascism in the USSR. How could people display such spontaneous joy and solidarity if there was oppression? Why do they love their leaders so much? In the evening there were special concerts and dances; Moscow was brilliantly illuminated, and was most beautiful and pleasing to the eye.

Vaikuntha Vasan rebutted the popular myth of visitors being shown only places pre-planned by Soviet authorities. The Ceylon delegation in fact were asked what places they would like to see when they arrived in Moscow. And there were no secret-service men - KGB - following the visitors; as widely made to believe in the West. It was only due to the language difficulties that visitors had to engage interpreters in the USSR.

The first place the delegation visited was the Moscow University, the most arresting, tallest and imposing of all the buildings in Moscow. Consisting of 21,000 rooms, 150 kilometres of corridors, 32 storeys; the University had 1,500 professors and 11,000 students attending the 11 faculties. Attendance at lectures was compulsory, and the average course was for five years. Graduating students were given jobs immediately.

The Moscow Metro underground stations were next on their itinerary. The marble constructed stations are nothing short of an art gallery describes Vaikuntha Vasan; the architecture and the beautiful frescoes on the walls depicting the new Soviet life. They also visited the imposing Kremlin Palace, where the Communist Party conferences and major assemblies convene; which was also the home of the famous Kremlin Museum. Vaikuntha Vasan was surprised to see every one of the 2500 seats occupied when he attended a Russian opera at the world famous Bolshoi Theatre. There were 30 large theatres in Moscow alone.

The delegation devoted a full day at the Pravda Publishing House-the premier media institution of USSR, which had the highest circulation of newspapers and magazines. Vaikuntha Vasan went to the Lenin Library, which housed 14 million volumes and manuscripts, and functioned as a national depository employing 1,500 staff. The library was open to all and there were no fees for using the library. Vaikuntha Vasan was fascinated to see the reader's order being sent by a conveyor belt and then the book being delivered by an electric train. The electric train doing a round every ten minutes.

Vaikuntha Vasan was greatly inspired when he visited the Lenin Museum, with exhibits and works spanning Lenin's entire life in great depth. Depicting Lenin's meeting with Stalin, his work among the workers, his imprisonment, periods of exile, his role in the 1917 revolution, his addresses to Congresses, the assassination attempt on his life, the several papers he edited and up to his death and the messages of condolence received. He said that it would take a whole month to see the various exhibits in the Lenin Museum; and a book to describe the effect on the visitor.

While in Moscow the delegation visited two factories. The first was a cigarette factory employing 2,300 workers, the production in which had increased five-fold since the revolution. The workers were found to be quick and energetic at their work and contended and happy in their jobs. The second was to the Stalin Automobile Plant and Works with a workforce of 5,000. Vaikuntha Vasan was amazed to see the most magnificent Palace of Culture for the workers, with several activities, the Palace Theatre itself comparing itself to that of the Royal Festival Hall of London. In fact all factories and works in the Soviet Union had a vast array of amenities in addition to the modern housing, free medical clinics, schools, libraries, canteens etc.

Vaikuntha Vasan was gratified to see the labour and employment conditions in the USSR highly organised to make the workers contended, happy and efficient. Article 118 of the Soviet Constitution guaranteed work for all and the right to work. There was no unemployment in the Soviet Union. Equal payment for equal work was the policy. Different production sectors had different grades of workers. Payment was either Time-payment method or Piece-work payment method. Some workers received larger salaries than the Ministers. There was no upper limit for salaries. The rent paid by the workers for housing was about 2-3% of the salary. Prices of commodities never rose; instead were slashed down several times.

The Museum for the Protection of Labour in Moscow displayed the ingenious devices and measures adopted by the government to protect the workers. People were the most treasured and valued capital in USSR. It staggered the imagination, Vaikuntha Vasan noted, to see the infinite care with which the conditions of workers were continuously improved.

As requested by the Ceylon delegation, a visit was arranged to Georgia, an Asian Republic of the USSR. They arrived at Tibilisi, the capital of Georgia, after brief stops at Kharkov (Ukraine), Rostov(Russia), and Suhumi(Georgia).

Vaikuntha Vasan went to see the Avlabar Printing Press, the underground printing house organised by the revolutionary leaders including Stalin. He was struck by the secret methods used in establishing and carrying out the printing press for three and a half years, until the Tsarist police discovered it, after several unsuccessful attempts. They later went to the town of Gori, where Stalin was born and visited the house where he lived for four years till 1883.They also visited a school where they found the children neatly dressed, healthy, smart and very active. The relationship between the teachers and students they noticed to be very cordial. They visited a hosiery factory producing cotton, silk and artificial silk stockings. Ninety nine percent of the 3,000 workers there were women.

The Ceylon delegation was taken by train to Natanabai near the Black Sea to see a collective farm producing tea, lemons, citrus and linseed. Even though the entire collective farm land belongs to the State, the use of the land is free. They are under the general direction of the Ministry of Agriculture and the Central Board of Collective Farms; and the farm pays an income tax varying between 1% - 5%.

Vaikuntha Vasan had made an extensive and objective study of the Soviet citizen's life in the USSR: Everybody is employed and literate. Education and Health Services were free. Sanatoriums and health resorts, were not only well equipped but were found everywhere we went. Theatres, cinemas, parks, palaces of culture and libraries were in abundance, with maximum scope for cultural advancement. I have seen people in prayer and worship-there was absolute freedom for religions. Freedom to criticise acts of government was evident from the large number of critical letters published in the newspapers. Women were not discriminated as to employment or pay. Fifty different nationalities lived in harmony in the USSR; each proud of their own language and culture with highest respect and regard for the other's language and culture; and this impressed me most, he said.

On the eve of the departure from the USSR a press conference and farewell party was organised. The delegates of the Ceylon delegation gave spirited speeches. Vaikuntha Vasan had earlier given a speech over the Moscow Radio: It is only after a visit to the Soviet Union that one can realise the terrific nature of the criminal propaganda that is being carried out in the capitalist countries against the Soviet Union. Every Soviet citizen I met fervently desired peace and friendship with all people of the world. The Soviet children are taught to love and respect all people, whether they are dark, brown or white. They are building more factories and intensifying their agricultural methods.

Their scientists are marching towards the conquest of nature and their aim is to utilise all scientific inventions for the benefit of man. In every field of human activity they are motivated by the sole desire to increase the happiness and prosperity of their people.

The farewell party went on till 4 am in the morning and vodka was flowing that night. After the dinner there was music and dance where the waitresses also joined. Thanking the Soviet friends and hosts the Ceylon delegation said good-bye to Russia, and proceeded to Vienna.

Congress of the Peoples for Peace

The Vienna Congress of the Peoples for Peace held from 12th to 19th December 1952 was a historic event with worldwide importance. Presided over by Prof. Frederic Joliet-Curie, 1800 delegates attended representing each and every of the 85 countries of the world. Vaikuntha Vasan was gratified to have met or listened to International personalities such as Dr. Hewlett Johnson (the Dean of Canterbury), Dr. J. C. Kumarappa (Gandhian economist), Ilya Ehrenburg (famous Russian author), Madame Sun-Yat sen (Chinese leader), Dr. Wirth (former German Chancellor), Prof. Pavlov (President of the Bulgarian Academy), Sr. Giuseppe Nitti (Italian Liberal leader) and many others. The venue was the magnificent Konserthaus concert hall situated in the British zone of Vienna. Vienna was at that time divided into five zones: the US, Soviet, British, French and International. The Ceylon delegation stayed in the French sector, but had meals in the US sector and attended the conference in the British sector.

The World Council of Peace met in July 1952 presided over by

Professor Joliet-Curie and set the pace for the Congress of the Peoples for Peace. 67 million people had already died in the first 50 years of the 20th century due to wars. Horrible acts had been committed by the dropping of atomic bombs and the use of bacteriological warfare. Great Art personalities Picasso and Matisse solicited worldwide support for a peace conference. The clamour for peace had also gathered in various forms all over Europe with assemblies in Berlin and Essen in Germany; Oslo (Norway), France, Poland, Italy and USA culminating in the Vienna Congress. The Asian and Pacific Peace Conference, which concluded in Beijing was one such notable event. The World Council for Peace held in Paris in 1949 had already resolved that the principal forces for peace were to be found among the men and women who suffered from war and without whose consent war would be impossible.

Address to the Governments of the Five Great Powers
The Congress of the Peoples for Peace, meeting at Vienna, December 12th, 1952, called on the Governments of the Five Great Powers, the U.S.A., the U.S.S.R., Great Britain, the People's Republic of China, and France, on whom so largely depends the peace of the world; at once to start negotiating to conclude a Pact of Peace...

The Congress of the Peoples for Peace in its statement said:
The necessity of renouncing the use of force as a means of settling international conflicts becomes daily ever more urgent...
We call for all hostilities in Korea to cease immediately and also for the immediate ending of hostilities in Viet Nam, Laos, Cambodia and Malaya, with unqualified respect for the right to independence of the peoples concerned... The Congress of the Peoples for Peace proclaims the right of all peoples to self-

determination and to choose their own way of life without any interference in their internal affairs, whatever motive be invoked in justification. The national independence of every state constitutes the essential condition of peace.

We protest against all racial discrimination, which is an insult to the human conscience that aggravates the danger of war.

We have heard the reports on the use of bacteriological warfare, made by famous experts, from different countries, which went to Korea and China. Deeply concerned by these reports, we categorically demand the immediate prohibition of biological warfare and the adherence of all states to the Geneva Protocol of 1925. The great achievements of science must not become a means to destroy millions of defenceless human beings. At the same time we demand an absolute ban on atomic, chemical and all other means of exterminating civil populations.

We hold that the Charter of the United Nations offers a guarantee of security for all the countries of the world but this Charter is being infringed in spirit and letter. We urge that the People's Republic of China be enabled to take its rightful seat at the United Nations. We urge likewise the admission of the fourteen nations who have as yet been unable to raise their voices there.

We urge, finally, that the United Nations become once more a place for finding agreement between the governments and not disappoint for much longer the hopes reposed in it by all the peoples of the world. The Peoples long to live in peace. whatever their regimes or loftiest ideals. War is hated by every people; war throws its shadow over every cradle. It is in the power of the peoples to change the course of events, to give back to mankind its confidence in a peaceful tomorrow.

We call on the peoples of the world to struggle for the spirit of negotiation and agreement, for the right of man to peace.

With a successful Vienna Peace Congress, Vaikuntha Vasan concluded his three months of his tour of China, Soviet Union and Austria discovering in fullness the sacred decree:

Peace can and must be saved!

Left:
In full head-gear outside the renowned **Red Square** in Moscow.

Below:
Viewing the magnificent **Kremlin Palace**, Moscow; with Vaikuntha Vasans are: (l-r): Sri Lankan Socialist leaders Shanmugathasan, Philip Gunawardena and S.D.Bandaranaike.

Right:
Malaysian
Prime Minister
**Tunku Abdul
Rahman** and
his wife recei-
ving Vaikuntha
Vasan in Kuala
Lumpur,
1975.

Vaikuntha Vasan (back row- third from left) was the first Asian to join the
Zambian Judicial Service. Photo taken with Judicial colleagues
in 1971.

Left: Still a staunch socialist; Vaikuntha Vasan addressing the Trotsky Memorial Seminar at Frankfurt, November 1979.

Face to face with the eminent civil lawyer **Lord Denning** (Baron of Whitchurch) in a reception in Kuala Lumpur in1975.

Indian Prime Minister **Indira Gandhi** seen here accepting Vaikuntha
Vasan's plea on behalf of the Tamils of Sri Lanka

Defence Minister **R.Venkataraman**(later, President of India) perusing
through Vaikuntha Vasan's Memorandum,1980.

On the campaign trail in 1979; Vaikuntha Vasan with **Atal Behari Vajpayee**, then External Affairs Minister of India.

Clarifying a point to the ardently listening Tamilnadu Chief Minister **M.Karunanithy**, in Chennai, Feb 1980.

Vaikuntha Vasan in the Pondicherry State of India (former French territory), leading a delegation of Tamil activists; and met with the Chief Minister **Rama -chandran.** Background is the portrait of south India's Illustrious hero late **Annadurai.**

On the campaign trail Vaikuntha Vasan also met the Education Minister of Pondicherry State, above left, in 1980.

Left:
Vaikuntha Vasan's campaign schedule even included the Vatican City. Seen with the **Pope John Paul II**outside the Vatican, 1983; where Vaikuntha Vasan presented a Memorandum on the plight of the Tamils of Sri Lanka.

Below:
A Family of talents- Vaikuntha Vasan's son Gandeepan-the artisit prodigy, with **Prince Charles** in 1985; when his portrait of former British Prime Minister Harold Macmillan was unveiled.

A quiet word-concurring with the Earl of Stockton (former British Prime Minister, **Harold Macmillan**), November 1985.

Vaikuntha Vasan beaming with delight, surrounded by his family on his 80th birthday, April 2000. left to right: daughter-in-law Anna, wife Maheswary, granddaughter Veena, son Gandeepan and grandson Misha.

Chapter 8

Sri Lanka and the Tamils
A Concise History

The most incomprehensible thing
About the world is that
It is comprehensible
-Albert Einstein

Current perspectives on contemporary Sri Lankan history are synonymous with the saga of the Tamil struggle that had dominated the attention of the international audience in the past two decades. But more prominent within this state of affairs is the incomprehensibility and the tumultuous nature of the grasp, of the entire episodes, by the world public at large. Although a vast majority are well aware of the conflict in Sri Lanka; nearly all of them cannot comprehend as to what is and has been really happening in that pearl of the Indian Ocean. There has been confusing, and incessantly chaotic volumes of output that had poured out;cluttered, muddled and incapacitated the minds of the public. Every endeavour is made here to present the whole story of this Island Nation in an absorbing and concise form; and in a clear and simple style; for effortless comprehension by one and all.

Fact File on Sri Lanka

Official name: The Democratic Socialist Republic of Sri Lanka

Island by many names: Sri Lanka/Lanka/Lankapuri (the resplendent island in Sanskrit/Pali);
Ilankai (Tamil for Lanka); Tamaraparani (a river in the south of Tamilnadu in the proximity of Lanka); Taprobane (Greek for Tamaraparani); Serendib (ascribed by the Moors meaning Cheran Theevu- Chera King's Island) and Ceylon (used by the Portuguese).
Ealam or Eelam: although denotes Sri Lanka; but is also used to denote the Tamil homelands.
Tamil Ealam: Official name adopted since 1976 to denote the north and east of Sri Lanka, the traditional homelands of the Tamils.

Names of praise: Pearl of the Indian Ocean, Pendant in the chain of India, The other Eden, The demi paradise, Tea gardens of the world, etc.

Location: South of India and separated by the Palk Strait with the narrowest point being 22 miles; 6 to 10 degrees north of equator and a latitude of 79 to 81 degrees east.
Area: 66,000Sq km (25,332 sq. miles) - almost the size of Ireland or Sierra Leone.
Population: 18.5 millions (1998).
Ethnicity: Sinhalese (74%), Tamils (19%), Muslims(7%).
Religions:Buddhism (69%), Hinduism (16%), Christianity (8%) and Islam (7%).

Island of Two Nations

Sri Lanka is an Island of Two Nations: the Sinhalese and the Tamils; with varying demographic percentages published at different times. The most simple population figures are found in the Fact File above. It is noteworthy that immediately after

Independence in 1948, the ratio of the Sinhalese was 67% to 26% Tamils. The distortions in the demographic statistics are explainable to the compelling shifts of populations that ensued.

The shifting demographic pattern was more due to:

(a) The disenfranchisement and subsequent repatriation of Tamils to India of Tamils from the Tea/Rubber Plantations.

(b) The displacement of a few hundred thousands of war affected Tamils to India – who are now returning back to Sri Lanka, and

(c) Another few hundred thousand Tamils that fled to Europe, North America and Australasia, following the state spon sored pogrom of 1983.

The nearest similarity to that of Sri Lanka is the Island of Cyprus, another Island of two Nations; situated in the Mediterranean. Both were ex-colonies of Britain locked up with incessant bloody conflicts. In Cyprus, the Greeks are the majority, inhabiting the southern part of the Island (likewise the majority Sinhalese occupying the southern Sri Lanka); and the Turks – the minority living in the northern part. The Cypriot Turks have affinity to mainland Turkey in the north; and as a parallel the Tamils who inhabit the north and east of Sri Lanka have closeness to the Indian mainland. Another incredible similarity but also an irony was that Turkey successfully intervened in 1975 to safeguard the Turkish Cypriots; whereas the Sri Lankan Tamils miserably botched up a rare opportunity when India intervened in 1987 to safeguard them from a spate of carpet bombings and economic blockade. The Turkish Cypriots are enjoying unparalleled freedom with the mainland Turkish army in occupation in north Cyprus. Whereas the Tamils of Sri Lanka, are scattered and torn apart; with fatigue and devastation.

Perplexity of the Origins

There have been endless disputes between the Sinhalese and the Tamils as to who came first to the Island; as though 'to have been first' would give the exclusive right to demand the possession of the Island. And there has also been confusion as to the origins of the Sinhalese race, as well as to the sovereignty issues of who ruled over whom.

The theory of the Sinhala Aryan migration to Sri Lanka preceding the Tamil Dravidian, which was concocted by Sinhalese extremists from time to time, has been now quashed as false by many historians. What is also clear is that the Sinhalese as claimed by them are not Aryans by any stretch of imagination; when even in India a rigid Aryan-Dravidian divide has lost its validity. The Sinhala Buddhist claim to Aryan race was purely based on the unwavering affinity attached to Lord Buddha (who was considered to be of Aryan Stock); And a proud claim to belong to his lineage.

The 'who came first to Sri Lanka' dispute has definitely come to a clear and logical end with the recent discoveries made by the Indian and international oceanographers, archaeologists and geologists, prominently led by British author-researcher Graham Hancock and Indian scientist Dr. Badrinarayan, (India's National Institute of Ocean Technology)and their team. The findings are copiously documented in Graham Hancock's masterpiece: ***Underworld – Flooded Kingdoms of the Ice Age*** and also televised in UK's Channel Four in early 2002.

One of the findings from this exploration is straight and simple: that the Indian mainland and the present Sri Lanka has been one land mass at least 10,600 years ago. The Island had broken away from the Indian mainland in stages and finally detached itself 4,800 years ago. The fact that archaeological proof of

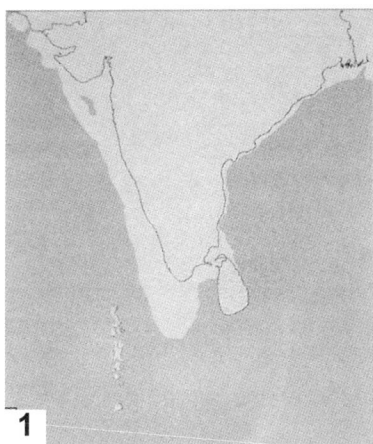

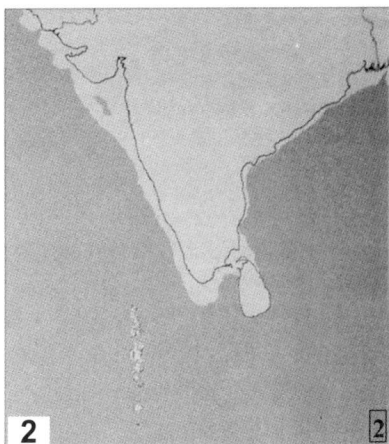

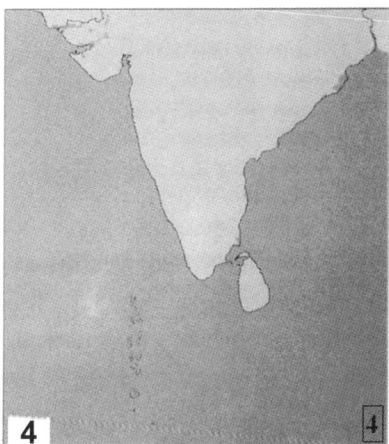

1. India 21,300 years ago: with the southern Kumari Kandam, western Dwaraka landmass and a larger Maldives archipelago.

2. India 16,400 years ago: Sri Lankan Island still part of the landmass; And a receding Kumari Kandam in the south.

3. India 10,600 years ago: Sri Lanka still connected; and the western and southern civilisations submerged under sea.

4. India 4,800 years ago: Sri Lanka detached and Maldives archipelago under sea, with only tiny islands surviving.

ancient civilisations dating back to 9,500 years ago have been
discovered in the west coast of India's Gulf of Cambay linked
to Dwaraka; and subsequently further underwater civilisation
discovered off Mahabalipuram and Poompuhar in the
Coromandel coast; has opened the Pandora's Box full of aston-
ishing surprises and findings for the explorers and for the historians. Graham Hancock asserted to the world at large: "World
History has to be rewritten now!; We can no longer think of the
so-called Fertile Crescent of Sumeria as the cradle of civilisation." And Monty Halls, ex-major in the Royal Marines, who
accompanied Hancock, and who had led the expedition for the
Scientific Exploration Society said: "I have never seen anything
like the majestic underwater structures of Mahabalipuram in
my 17 years of diving !".

The predecessors of both the Tamils and the Sinhalese have
lived in the attached and detached parts of what is now Sri
Lanka is therefore a certainty. As a natural inference then, the
subsequent waves of maritime migrations would have only
interbred with the earlier inhabitants, who were ancient Tamils:
the Nagas, Yakkas and Veddas. Nagas were an ancient and
powerful Dravidian race that attached much significance to the
Cobra-the Dravidian emblem of Earth. Their presence was
found all over India including the Indus Valley Civilisation. A
powerful warrior people, they left their impressions in various
forms - places like: Nagadipa(the holy Island off Jaffna peninsula), Nagapattinam, Nagaland, Nagpur etc. People like: the
Nayars of Kerala(Nagars) who give prominence to the Cobra
emblem; names like Nagaram or Nagar(a town-where Nagas
lived). Yakkas too were Dravidians with super human talents,
with possible descent from the Rakshasas of Ravana, the
Emperor of Lanka (circa. 5,000 B.C.). They were accredited to
have built the magnificient irrigation tanks in the Island, only
possible, then, by super intelligent and powerfully built people.

Veddas were hunters and cultivators of arid land agriculture (chenas); and are linked to Valli, the princess who was invested to Skanda, the warrior prince incarnation of Lord Muruga in Kathirkamam. Veddas, who are descendents of the ancient Dravidian tribes of South India, are also considered to be of Tamil origin.

The Tamil lands in the north and east of Sri Lanka are only a natural extension of the ancient Tamil Nadu. The Poompuhar civilisation in the east of India was connected to the Jaffna peninsula. The great Kumari Kandam(submerged) in the south, famed for the first two Tamil Sangams (Tamil Literary Academies) is no more mythology. (See maps in page127). The third and the final Tamil Sangam (circa. 2500 B.C. to 200 B.C.) was centred in the present city of Madurai. The high resolution inundation mapping-a cutting edge science that has been used by world's leading geological expert Dr. Glenn Milne,of Durham University(UK) has now discovered these antediluvian civilisations prior to the Last Glacial Maximum(LGA-denotes the flooding of lands due to rising sea level between 17,000 and 2,000 years ago). Indian Sages have termed such oceanic bed upheavals as Pralayas. Augmented to the above mapping is the under-water discovery by Graham Hancock, of a contiguous landmass with advanced archaeological monuments. All this goes to establish that Tamil language and civilisation as the most ancient in known human history. And also dispels the hitherto dispute of 'who came first to Sri Lanka'.

The Buddhist chronicle Mahavamsa, claim that the Sinhalese are descendents of the exiled prince Vijaya, and his 700 followers from the city of Sinhapura in Bengal; who found refuge in Lanka in 483 BC. Prince Vijaya married Kuweni, a Yakka princess who spoke a broken form of Tamil and ruled the north west of the Island. His second wife, a Tamil Pandyan princess came from Madurai; along with 700 Tamil Pandyan girls and married prince Vijaya's followers. Vijaya is said to have reno-vated the five Ishwarams dedicated to Lord Shiva including Thirukoneswaram in Trincomalee, Munneswaram in Chilaw, and Thiruketheeswaram in Mannar. The Sinhalese population nevertheless had evolved from a continuous flux of different ethnic groups from India. The Elu dialect, a corrupt form of the Tamil language of the Yakkas, catalysed with Pali, Sanskrit, Telugu and Tamil to produce the Sinhala language.

Even after the detachment from the mainland, Sri Lanka had strong south Indian influence, especially cultural, political and commercial links. But the spread of Buddhism into Sri Lanka during emperor Ashoka's period exerted an even greater impact on the indigenous population. Ashoka's envoys Prince Mahinda(247 B.C.) and later Princess Sangamitta(207 B.C.) introduced Buddhism into Sri Lanka. The Anuradhapura king-dom of the newly evolved Sinhalese kings (3rd century BC to 10th century AD) was moulded along Buddhist tradition start-ing from Devanampiya Tissa. Anuradhapura is situated in the north central province of the Island.

The repeated conquests of, and rule over, most of Sri Lanka by the Tamil Kings of the mainland from time to time had made an adverse impact on the Sinhalese psyche. The Mahavamsa(a chronicle written in Pali by Mahanama, a Buddhist monk) has reference to one of these conquests. In the second century BC, Ellala, an aristocrat from the Chola dynasty, conquered and ruled Sri Lanka righteously, from its Anuradhapura headquar-ters for 44 years. The son of the defeated king (who had become a loyal vassal), defied his father and fled to the Ruhuna jungles in the south. There he raised an army and won in the historic battle against Ellala-the Tamil King. The renegade was Duttu Gemunu; who legend said, as a boy used to sleep crouching his

body within a confined space. When one day his mother wor-
riedly asked why he stooped and slept in such a manner;
whereas the bed was large enough? Duttu Gemunu replied:
"How on earth could I spread my legs and sleep when the
Tamils are crushing me from the north and there is the sea in the
south?" - a fear-resentment complex that could fittingly be
termed as the Duttu Gemunu psyche.

Later again with the ascent of Chola power in India;and with
the instability of the kingdom of Anuradhapura, the Cholas
ruled over the entire Island from 993AD to 1070AD. The powerful Chola Empire had in fact reigned over the whole of south
east Asia; extending across the Malayan and Indonesian archipelago upto and including Cambodia in the east. The Chola
realm flourished in the Island in architecture, arts, administration, irrigation works and trade, basing their capital at
Polannaruwa, situated in the north east region of the Island. It
was Vijayabahu (1055-1110), who after having smoothly inte-
grated the Tamil settlements, capitalised on the decline of Chola
power in the mainland to recapture the seat of power of the
Cholas in Polannaruwa. Culavamsa, another chronicle in the
Pali language, quotes Parakramabahu I (1153AD-1186AD), a
king with a mixed Tamil-Sinhala parentage, as a hero who kept
the Tamil rule at bay; and brought the whole Island under his
reign with Polannaruwa as the capital.

Despite the passing references in the Mahavamsa and the
Culavamsa chronicles both obsessed with doctoring history to
gratify Sinhala heroism and displaying traces of anti-Tamil
sentiments; the continuing flux of the Tamil and Sinhalese populations had maintained remarkable harmony. A continuous
migration of south Indian armies, artisans and priests arrived in
various parts of Sri Lanka at various periods; and always at the
invitation of the local rulers. The Sinhalese kingdoms very

often recruited armies and mercenaries from the Tamil kingdoms in the mainland; to wage internal wars and for the defence
of their kingdoms. Similarly the Tamil Pandyan kingdom had
regular alliances with the Sinhalese Kingdom, not only in their
wars against the Tamil Cholas, but also of the matrimonial
nature and of providing with bloodline rulers. Even statutes and
treasury accounts in the Island kingdoms were maintained in
Tamil and the signatures of the kings were in Tamil.

The Kingdom of Polannaruwa started to decline following the
death of Parakramabahu-I (1153AD-1186AD). His costly
adventure following the invasion and the complete rout of his
entire army at the hands of the Pandyan King was one of the
causes for the decline. The other was the overstretched irrigation and construction works for which he had to raise taxes
resulting in discontent.

With the rise of the power of the Kalinga kingdom in the mainland, Magha (the princely son of the Kalinga king
Manuvarathan), conquered the Island with a large Dravidian
army of Tamils and Keralas in 1215. He then consolidated his
rule in Polannaruwa and went on to set up strong littoral out-
posts to prevent invasions. His rule lasted forty years till 1255,
during which time he actively patronised the Shaiva religion.
His rule also led to the decentralisation of the powers of the
Polannaruwa kingdom. The surviving chiefs of Polannaruwa
retreated to the remote jungle areas and set up centres of resistance. Vijayabahu III – one of the chieftans, organised his rule in
Dambadeniya in the south and in the districts of Vanni.

Vanni is synonymous to the present northern Tamil areas consisting of 18 Vanni territories designated within the Vavuniya,
Mannar and Trincomalee districts. The Vanni chieftans who

were descendents of the Tamil warriors recruited by the Kings, belonged to the Vanniyar caste from the mainland. They set up their autonomous principalities from this period (13th century) onwards. The Eastern littoral-commonly known as the Batticoloa region- in south of Tricomalee and Mahaweli Ganga river delta; down to Kumuna and the Kumbukkan Oya river were also ruled by Vanni chieftans; as was in the western coast of Puttalam. Both the eastern and western Vanniyars were Mukkuvars (Tamil caste observing matrilineal customs) of Malabar extraction.

With the descent of the Kalinga rule and that of Magha; Parakramabahu II, the son of Vijayabahu III assumed power in Polannaruwa for a brief period. But with the invasion of the Island by Chandrabanu from the Malay peninsula and later with the growth of power of the Arya Chakravarthis in Jaffna, originating from the Pandya kingdom; ensued the decline of the Sinhala dynasty based in Polannaruwa. The seeds were now sown for the three distinct kingdoms: Jaffna(North), Kandyan(Central)and Kotte(South and West-Maritime).

The Arya Chakravarthis became a powerful dynasty, based in the majestically laid out Nallur Rajadhani, in Jaffna, from the 13th century; the first king being Vijaya Koolankai. Their power occasionally spread over the whole Island often invading the Sinhala kingdom first based in Kurunegala, which later moved to Gampola in the southern hill country. Subsequently the Gampola kingdom moved towards the western fortification of Kotte, near Colombo. A south Indian general Alakeswara who was entrusted in the building of the kingdom in Kotte; also fought and defended against the Arya Chakravarthi king of Jaffna.

Meanwhile in the central hill country, the Kandyan kingdom sought during Rajasimha I's (1581-93) period, noble pantarams from Kerala, who later became the princely Bandaras. And formed matrimonial alliances with the rulers in Madurai. The Kandyan kingdom also became closely tied to the Temple of the Buddha's Tooth relic. There was also an influx of Shaivite holymen into the districts of Kandyan kingdom, while Rajasimha I actively practised the Shaiva religion.

Foreign Rule

At the time of the arrival of the Portuguese in the Island of Ceylon in 1505 there were hence three distinct Kingdoms: a Tamil Kingdom in the north based in Jaffna; and two Sinhala Kingdoms – one in the western and southern maritime country with Kotte as the capital; and the second in the central hill country with Kandy as its capital. Portuguese, the first western colonial power to arrive in the Island made their first appearances, near Colombo, searching for exotic spices and gems. It was Vasco da Gama who pioneered the discovery of the Orient following the discovery of the Cape of Good Hope in South Africa. But the Moors had already superseded them and were in control of the spice and gem trade.

An interesting legend hilariously depicts the first arrival of the Portuguese thus: The king of Kotte having been informed by some of his citizens of spotting a ship with aliens of bleached complexion (the Portuguese) and huge tubes (artillery) sending thundering blasts (salvos); sent forth his envoys to receive the surprise visitors. The over cautious Kotte king had ordered the visitors to be brought in a long winded-circuitous route to Kotte; which was merely a few miles from the coast of Colombo. The cunning Portuguese had their own way of tracking their delegation. Intermittently the ship's captain fired salvos from the ship so that the distance of the ship's anchorage from the Kotte kingdom could be estimated by the delegation on journey. The more they walked they kept hearing the canon blasts in symmetrical range from their base ship! The

Portuguese soon knew that the capital of the kingdom was not that far away! And so decided to invade the Kotte kingdom in 1505.

In the north, the kingdom of Jaffna was immersed in a golden era of Tamil Shaiva culture and prosperity under King Para Rajasekaram (1478-1519). His successor Sankili I (1519-1561) managed to repulse the Portuguese with the support of the Vijayanagara chieftains of south India. But Mannar in the northwest came under the Portuguese, plagued by ruthless conversion of the Tamil inhabitants into the Roman Catholic religion. Following a century of resistance, the Portuguese captured the Jaffna kingdom in 1619, which was then ruled by Sankili II. Hinduism thereafter suffered a sharp decline with most Hindu temples and practices destroyed. Portuguese thereafter consolidated their maritime rule of the Island with ease.

The Dutch who followed the Portuguese were attracted to the Island while on their trade route to the East Indies and China. The Kandyan kings made mutual alliances with the Dutch with the view of overthrowing the Portuguese from the Island. Eventually the Dutch gained supremacy over the Portuguese with the support of the Kandyan kingdom in 1656. They then consolidated the maritime provinces and ejected the Portuguese out of the Island; and continued to govern exclusively till 1796. One of the major achievements under the Dutch rule was the codification in 1707 of the customary laws of the Tamils (evolved under the Jaffna kings); named as Thesavalamai. *The law of Thesavalamai* is an ideal fusion of the matriarchal and of the patriarchal social systems. Along with this the Dutch also compiled the Thombus(land titles). In the Singhalese areas the Dutch introduced the Roman-Dutch law.

The Kandyan kingdom meanwhile became the citadel of Singhala culture and traditions; free from both the Portuguese and Dutch rule. But the fascinating feature of the Kandyan kingdom was the active solicitation and fusion of the south Indian Nayakkar royalties and warriors from Madurai with the Kandyan ruling elite. In so much that a brother of a Nayakkar-descent queen in Kandy, Sri Vijaya Rajasimha, was enthroned as the king of Kandy in 1739. This was then the fountain of the Nayakkar dynasty in Sri Lanka and also the last independent ruling dynasty of the Island. His successor Kirti Sri Rajasimha (1747-1782) was a staunch Shaivite prominently adorning the holy ash on his forehead;but actively promoting the Buddhist religion and culture. Sri Vikrama Rajasimha his successor, the last king of Kandy failed to exert proper control of the kingdom leading to a revolt by his chiefs who betrayed him to the British. The outgoing king Sri Vikrama Rajasimha along with his chiefs signed the Treaty of 1815 with the British in the Tamil language.

The British East India Company, which had already obtained a foothold in India, administered the maritime provinces of the Island from Madras (Chennai) between 1796 and 1802. In 1802 Britain established the Island as a colony of the Crown, under the Treaty of Amiens(1802) ousting the Dutch from Ceylon. With the ceding of the Vanni chiefdoms in the north ruled by the defiant Vanni Prince Pandara Vanniyan in 1803 and that of the Kandyan kingdom in 1815;the British began consolidating the maritime Sinhala and the Tamil areas and unified the erstwhile three kingdoms into a unified unit in 1833; as recommended by the Colebrook Commission, and established the Government of Ceylon. A severe change in the history of Ceylon had now taken place whereas the Sinhalese and the Tamils of the Island came under one rule. In the same year a Legislative Council was also established in Colombo.

Having survived a great rebellion in 1817 in Kandy to get rid of the British; the British also survived another rebellion in 1848 in Kandy against the imposition of punitive taxes. From 1830s onwards the British established commercial coffee plantations in the upcountry with imported cheap labour from south India. The British and their recruiting agents lured the Tamils from nearer districts in India with mis-selling inducements of utopian promises. Wherein the Sinhalese refused to do the coolie work to transform and work on the plantations, the Tamils were settled in mountain slopes on slum like terraced lines to churn out the wealth for British entrepreneurs. The demographic pattern of the upcountry was also dramatically changed with this import of the Tamil labour force, resulting in contempt and resentment by the up-country (Kandyan) Sinhalese population.

A cultural and religious revivalism occurred in the North and in the South during the mid 19th century. Arumuga Navalar (1822-1879), a writer and publisher, brought about a revivalism of the orthodox Shaivite religion and successfully defended against the Christian missionaries from converting the Tamils. Jaffna and the Batticoloa regions thus regained their stronghold of the orthodox form of Shaivaite Hinduism. In the South, Anagarika Dharmapala (1864-1933), a journalist, spearheaded the Sinhala Buddhist revivalism through his newspaper Sinhala Baudhaya founded in 1906. In 1911 he declared: *the country of the Sinhalese shall be governed by the Sinhalese.*

Communal, religious and racial 'Riots' are a phenomenon art fully nurtured and manipulated by western colonial agencies as one of their tools to disrupt national unity, societies and the working classes. The Island experienced its first 'modern-age style riots' in 1915, when the Sinhalese attacked the Moors. The

Moors are Muslims; who were descendents of traders from the Malabar and Tamilnadu's Coramandel coast. They interbred with the local community and became the Tamil speaking Moors. With the arrival of the Portuguese who were rivalling with the Moors in commerce; the Moors felt threatened and sought refuge in the central Kandyan kingdom and served the kingdom through their expertise in trade. For the services rendered the Kandyan kings, later bequeathed agricultural lands to the Moors in the proximity of the Eastern province. There is now a considerable concentration of Moors in selective areas of Eastern province;and in pockets of western and central provinces.

The riots against the Muslim traders was provoked as the Sinhala traders accused the former of practising unfair competitive methods (extending easy credit terms, charging exorbitant prices etc). The British over-reacted by imprisoning the Sinhalese political leaders including the Senanayakas. Sir Ponnambalam Ramanathan (a Tamil and the first member to be elected on the 'educated Ceylonese' seat in the Legislative Council) criticised the Government for this over-reaction; travelled up to London and obtained the release of the imprisoned leaders. On his return to Colombo, the Sinhalese gave Sir P Ramanathan a tumultuous welcome and placed him in a chariot and pulled the chariot around the city of Colombo! The Tamil speaking Moors have to this day not forgiven the Jaffna Tamils for this act of partiality towards the Sinhalese.

In 1911, the Legislative Council included for the first time local inhabitants to be represented as 'Unofficial members'. Following this the Ceylon National Congress, the first political party of the Island was formed in 1919, along the lines of the Indian National Congress, with the Sinhalese (both low-country and up-country) and the Tamils, of the English educated elite class, joining hands. They united to seize constitutional powers from the hesitant British imperialists. The founders included theTamil leaders Sir P. Ramanathan and his brother Sir P. Arunachalam; and the Sinhalese leaders D. S. Senanayake, S.W.R.D. Bandaranyake and J. R. Jayawardena (all three later became Prime Ministers). Between 1921 and 1924 the number of 'Unofficial members' (Ceylonese) in the Legislative council was increased; and Tamils even sought election from the Sinhalese majority Colombo seat. The socio-cultural amity among the Sinhalese and the Tamils at all levels and at all times were cordial and free from any suspicion or hatred.

The first elected representative system was created following the Donoughmore Commission Report, which brought in the universal franchise elections in Ceylon. The Sinhalese leaders at first refused to fall for this proposal as they agreed with the Tamil leadership that this would only augment a majority domination over minority situation; and entered into an agreement with the Tamil leaders including Sir P. Ramanathan, to stipulate a just ratio of Sinhalese and Tamils, taking into consideration of the historical factor. But the Sinhalese later fell for the unsolicited gift of majority power and colluded with the British authorities in pushing through the Donoughmore Commission Report.

The Report was adopted in haste with a thin majority of 19 voting for and 17 voting against; and thus the Donoughmore Constitution came into being in 1931 with an elected Legislative State Council and a Board of Ministers.The prominent opposition came from the Tamil nationalist leader Sir P. Ramanathan. Despite being a national leader, Sir P. Ramanathan saw the first signs of Tamils losing their sovereignty, equality and identity with this sudden sweep of universal franchise. The first signs of fissure in national unity devel-

oped from thereon. The mutuality and friendship that the educated Sinhalese and Tamils had built over a period now stood
undermined. A disenchanted Sir P. Ramanathan summoned a
meeting of leading Tamils to his residence in Chunnakam,
Jaffna and warned the Tamils never to trust the Sinhalese and
more so the British authorities any more. For they had betrayed
the Tamils in haste, he accused; and the Tamils had no choice
but to boycott the elections of 1931. The British on the other
hand had utilised the hard working Tamils from the north in
large numbers to run the civil service, railways and also the
mercantile establishments; and the Plantation Tamils in their tea
and rubber estates to generate colossal profits. The deceitful
British had thus sowed the seeds for a turbulent future to an
Island Nation.

There were other developments that followed the universal
franchise of the Donoughmore Constitution. New political parties sprung up to field candidates to the Legislative Council.
They were: Lanka Sama Samaja Party (LSSP) a Trotskyite
party (1935); Sinhala Maha Sabha, the first covert Sinhala
party(1937) by S.W.R.D. Bandaranaike; Ceylon Communist
Party (1943) and the Tamil Congress(TC) by G.G.
Ponnambalam (1944). Ceylon National Congress (1919) was
converted as the United National Party(UNP) in 1946, under
the leadership of D.S.Senanayake.   Many leading Sinhalese
Christians like S.W.R.D. Bandaranaike got themselves recon-
verted to Buddhist religion to obtain the Buddhist votes. They
were amusingly branded as the 'Donoughmore Buddhists'.

In 1944, Whitehall appointed a Royal Commission under the
chairmanship of Viscount Soulbury. The Constitutional
Commission was constituted to draft a new Constitution for Sri
Lanka to enable it to march towards self-government. Once
again the Tamils and other minorities demanded that the

Constitution incorporate minority rights. The Tamils formed an ad-hoc body, which became the Tamil Congress; to make their representations before the Soulbury Commission. Their leader G.G.Ponnambalam erroneously put forward the fifty-fifty demand of equal representation (50% for Sinhalese and 50% for Tamils and other minorities), which was rejected outright as unreasonable.

D. S. Senanayake, the leader of the Ceylon National Congress hurriedly appealed to the Tamils: *Do you want to be governed from London or do you want, as Ceylonese, to help govern Ceylon?* And he continued: *On behalf of the Congress and on my own behalf, I give the minority communities the sincere assurance that no harm need they fear at our hands in a free Lanka.* And meanwhile a select committee of the State Council was appointed in 1945 to report on Sinhala and Tamil as official languages, following the adoption of a similar resolution a year hitherto. In 1946 the Select Committee reported positively on the transition from English to Sinhalese and Tamil as the Official languages.

Post Independent Ceylon

In the 1947 General Elections that followed the enactment of the Soulbury Constitution; the United National Party was returned to Parliament with D. S. Senanayake as the leader. A resolution was then drafted by the Cabinet formally requesting Britain to grant complete independence. The entire cabinet approved the draft including the Tamil Minister C. Suntheralingam (who stubbornly defied the boycott calls from the entire mainstream Tamil leadership). The British Parliament then enacted the Ceylon Independence Act in December 1947, and granted Independence on February 4th 1948. D.S.Senanayake became the first Prime Minister of Independent Sri Lanka. No sooner the country was given

Independence, the first move to be taken by the government ashamed the world polities: the stripping of citizenship and voting rights for the economy's backbone – the Tamil workers of the tea and rubber plantations. This was in fact the fore runner of more anti-Tamil legislations that were to follow suit. The Tamil Minister Suntheralingam did not remain in the cabinet for long; and later regretted deeply over his decision in supporting the cabinet draft - for he could have vetoed the resolution, thereby postponing the Independence Act until sufficient safeguards were granted.

The blatant betrayal of the Tamil people repeated itself; as the British Colonial Office had already in 1945 given into a request from D. S. Senanayake, when he visited London and secured a very special concession pertaining to the up-country Tamil plantation workers. The Tamil plantation workers brought into Ceylon by the British recruiting agents from 1830 onwards, had been the sole labour force, that cleared the thick jungles and created the plantations and produced first coffee and later tea and rubber for the profitable British plantation companies. Despite this, the British colluded with the right wing leader and had let the independent government deal with the fate of over one million Tamils of Indian origin on their citizenship status.

The hapless upcountry Tamils of Indian origin became a sitting target and were betrayed, of all people, by Ceylon Tamil leaders such as G. G. Ponnambalam.In return for cabinet positions they actively aided and supported the Sinhalese leadership to drivethrough theCitizenship Act and the Ceylon (Parliamentary Elections) Amendment Act both of 1948, disenfranchising over one million Tamils. Tamil leaders; S. J. V. Chelvanayagam and C.Vanniasingham felt disgusted at this gross betrayal by G.G.Ponnambalam; quit the Tamil Congress party and in 1949 formed the Federal Party (the predecessor to the Tamil United Liberation Front).

Concurrently on the economic front Sri Lanka had entered into a class conflict during the eve of its independence with the General Strike of 1947 and the rapid mobilisation of the working class forces against the capitalist government. The leftist parties under the leadership of great stalwarts of the calibre of Dr. N. M. Perera, Dr. Colvin R.de Silva, Dr. Wickremasinghe and Peiter Kuennemen had enthralled most of the working class population. The powerful Government Clerical Service Union (GCSU) of which Krishna Vaikuntha Vasan was the General Secretary; and the powerful People's Voice weekly, of which he was the editor-publisher supported the socialist movement with all its might. As is always the case in modern history; Economics is the root cause of all political history and as such also of conflicts and turmoil. The precipitous nature of calamity that overtook the Island Nation should therefore be viewed only through such a kaleidoscope. The socialist movement had already taken firm root since 1935-with the founding of the Lanka Sama Samaja Party(LSSP). Workers in all sectors; especially in the Tea and Rubber plantations were in a slave-like decadent state as to wages, housing and health. The British capitalists and the Sinhala mudalalis including the landed aristocracy, got the fright and were colluding for a while as to what needed to be done. And so the events were shaped accordingly.

Back to the political front; two developments grip the national leadership issue. S.W.R.D. Bandaranaike, the Oxford educated son of a maha mudaliar (principal chieftain) who having merged his Sinhala Maha Saba with the United National Party, saw no opening of becoming a leader in an already dynastically controlled outfit. The UNP was cynically called the Uncle Nephew Party with the Senanayakas and Kotelawalas wielding control along with J. R. Jeyawardena. S. W. R. D. Bandaranaike had already launched the Sinhala Maha Sabha in 1937 on the basis of rejuvenating the rural masses to take control of the Island Nation's affairs, anticipating the departure of the British. He along with other nationalist leaders sought to heal the many divisions endemic in the Sinhala society, such as the caste system and the low-country versus up-country divisions. He, being a low-country Sinhalese, chose to marry into an aristocratic Sinhalese family of the up-country. An eloquent orator in both Sinhala and English; S.W.R.D.Bandaranaike affirmed that he had the ability to lead the country and founded the Sri Lanka Freedom Party in 1951.

The next year D.S.Senanayake, the Prime Minister fell from a horse and ended his life, leaving the UNP in a state of mayhem, with his son Dudley Senanayake assuming power. The UNP was later re-elected in the general elections (1952). The upcountry plantation Tamil population having been disenfranchised could not vote in this election and therefore lost their 7 seats in a House of 95. In a grotesque manner their electorates were exploited to return additional Sinhalese M.Ps. The economic crises and the labour unrest with waves of strikes (Hartal) brought the right wing UNP into disrepute; and the fidgety Dudley Senanayake resigned in 1953 giving way to a flamboyant and rash Sir John Kotelawela, Senanayake's uncle, as the Prime Minister. Unable to coexist with the recoiling Kotelawela, G.G.Ponnambalam quit the cabinet as Minister of Industries and Fisheries; and withdrew his Tamil Congress party support to the UNP government. The Island's economic position worsened day by day; as it continued to depend on exporting cash crops, while importing consumer and luxury goods in large amounts. The country was now ripe for a diversion into a political crisis to avert a socialist revolution.

Sir John Kotelawela, the Prime Minister made a strategic visit to Jaffna in 1954 wooing support from the northern province. There he declared known that Sinhala and Tamil will become the official languages of the country. S.W.R.D. Bandaranaike who had by now begun mustering support for his newly founded Sri Lanka Freedom Party (SLFP), grabbed the opportunity and did a one-upmanship by announcing that his party will make Sinhala the only official language, with reasonable use of Tamil. L.H.Mettananda, Principal of Ananda College, Colombo and a Buddhist fundamentalist, and his cohorts orchestrated a movement to make Sinhala only the official language; converting a simple issue into a national crisis. The leftist parties supported the two-language formula; while the Buddhist clergy jumped into the fray and cried for Sinhala Only. Bewildered Sir John Kotelawela did a somersault and declared that his UNP government will make Sinhala only the official language of the country. Now it was the turn of S.W.R.D. Bandaranaike; who declared that he will not merely make Sinhala - the only official language but that too within 24 hours! The seed for a calamity to come during the next five decades had now been sowed with hot-headed brashness. The Federal Party (Tamil Arasu Kadchi) meanwhile demanded a federal set-up giving the Tamils an autonomous federal state in the North and East.

Running up to the general election of June 1956, the SLFP formed a People's United Front with allied parties under the banner of Mahajana Eksath Peramuna (M.E.P); which was swept to power with S.W.R.D. Bandaranaike becoming the Prime Minister. The Tamil Federal Party won 10 out of the 12 seats in the North and East. The upcountry Tamils deprived from voting were prevented again from electing any members to the Parliament. Sir John Kotelawela, the routed UNP leader, bolted to the safe haven of Kent, UK; where he was feted for the rest of his life with the luxuries of a merry batchelor. Back

to the home front- Hot on the heels of being elected,
Bandaranaike rushed through the Sinhala Only official language Act. Tamil M.Ps along with hundreds of Federal Party
cadres performed a Satyagraha (non-violent sit in demonstration) outside the Parliament. A hitherto socialist now turned
fascist, Philip Gunawardena mobilised buses; loaded them with
hooligans from his constituency; and let them loose on the
peacefully protesting Tamil leaders. Many leaders including the
subsequent leader of the TULF- Appapillai Amirthalingam-
were injured in the attack. The hooligans now on the loose
went from the Galle Face Green sea front towards the south and
north of Colombo attacking Tamil homes and businesses.
Similar riots also engulfed other areas including the Gal Oya
development scheme in the Eastern province where Sinhala
hoodlums were being settled under the colonisation programme
masterminded by the first Premier D.S.Senanayake. Fleeing
Tamil refugees were taken to refugee centres and the army was
called in to quell the riots. 1956 June thus witnessed the second
Riots of Sri Lanka-the first being the anti-Muslim Riots of
1915. Sri Lanka – a prosperous paradise of happily mixing
communities and peace- became an Island of hell from thereon.

The Tamil crises which had two dimensions; the disenfranchisement of one million up country Tamils (political)and the
forcing of Sinhala language as the only official language(politi
co-linguo) was worsened now with a third crisis – that of land
grabbing (economic) in the Tamil homelands. Bandaranaike's
Land development minister C. P. de Silva, vigorously continued
with the colonisation of the Tamil lands that was started by
D.S.Senanayake. Sinhalese were settled in vast numbers in
Vavuniya, and Padawiya in the north and Trincomalee and
Amparai(Gal Oya) in the East. The Tamil Federal Party met in
the naval base town of Trincomalee at its convention and
demanded that colonisation of the Tamil lands with Sinhalese
should be stopped forthwith. In July 1957 Bandaranaike nego-

tiated with the Federal Party agreeing to set up Regional Councils – a semi federal system- and to allow for reasonable use of Tamil language. Bandaranaike wanted to briskly implement his other election agendas-that of nationalisation of tea, rubber, buses, schools, petroleum etc. and the ejection of the British bases. Therefore, he was inclined to solve the crisis on the Tamil front. The negotiation with the leader of the Federal Party S.J.V.Chelvanayagam resulted in what was named the Bandarnaike-Chelvanayagam Pact (B-C Pact). The right wing J. R. Jeyawardena of the UNP now had his turn to do the one-upmanship. He did a long march to Kandy protesting against the B-C Pact. The Buddhist priests jumped into the fray again; this time physically inside the lawns of the Temple Trees official residence of the Prime Minister. Bewildered Bandaranaike unilaterally abrogated the B-C pact.

Meanwhile the enthusiastic Bandaranaike government was speedily implementing the Official Language Act; and did not even spare the motor vehicles bearing number plates with Roman alphabets. The government introduced the Sinhala alphabets on the vehicle number plates starting with a Sinhala Sri (the first word of Sri Lanka). The Tamil Federal Party objected to Sinhala number plated vehicles plying in north and east. Appapillai Amirthalingam, the youthful lieutenant of the Federal Party, launched the "anti-Sri" campaign in Jaffna in May 1958, by personally tarring the Sinhala Sri number plates on the nationalised Ceylon Transport Board buses that arrived in Jaffna. Tamil MPs who continued with this campaign were arrested and later released, amidst tensions on both sides. The Federal Party later organised a convention in Vavuniya, the border town, to resolve on a civil disobedience movement. As a backlash to these the government members scrupulously orchestrated an anti-Tamil riot; for the second time. The scale of violence was on a higher pitch and more widespread than of the 1956 Riots. Several hundred Tamils were killed in Colombo in the provinces, and over 10,000 made homeless. On the second day of the rioting the Indian High Commissioner urged a reluctant Bandaranaike to declare a State of Emergency. On the fourth day, Sir Oliver Goonetilleka, the Governor-General, stepped in and called out all the three armed services and declared a State of Emergency; lasting for several months. The homeless Tamils in and around Colombo were transported in a cargo ship - *The Lanka Rani*. The parting of the ways between the Tamils and the Sinhalese had now taken place. And in a desperate attempt to please the Tamils, Bandaranaike enacted the Tamil Language (Special Provisions)Act, allowing for reasonable use of Tamil; while the Tamil MPs were in house arrest and the Emergency was prevailing.

While all this was happening Bandaranaike had already upset and earned enemies of the mudalalis (capitalists) and foreign interests. He had nationalised the bus transport, petroleum companies, the port cargo companies, major tea and rubber plantations and brought in the redistribution of rice producing lands to small farmers. He did not stop there; for he expelled the British air base at Katunayake and the British naval base at Trincomalee at short notice. His fate had by now been decided by other than the Tamils with whom he was busily messing around. He was assassinated at his residence on September 25th, 1959, by a deranged Buddhist monk named Somarama Thero, who was later sentenced to death. The web of conspiracy was extensive, including two ex-ministers Stanley de Zoysa and Mrs Wimala Wijewardena being mentioned. The high priest of the Kelaniya Buddhist Temple, Buddharakita Thero was also sentenced with the charge of conspiring to murder. The SLFP was in disarray, left with a caretaker government under W. Dahanayake.

In 1960, the UNP regained power for a brief period without an overall majority; and then in a snap election the SLFP came back to power under the leadership of Sirimavo, the widow of the late Bandaranaike. Sirimavo Bandaranike created history as being the first woman Prime Minister of the world. One of her first acts was the nationalisation of schools, which were being mostly run by Catholic and Protestant missionaries with state aid. The Catholics mounted a disobedience movement and occupied their schools. At the bequest of the Indian Prime Minister Jawaharlal Nehru; Cardinal Gracias of Bombay hurried to Colombo; intervened and prevented a Buddhist-Catholic blood bath.

It was under Sirimavo Bandaranaike's period in 1961 that the Sri Lankan army was moved into the Northern Tamil province; as a reaction to the Federal Party's launching of a Satyagraha (civil disobedience movement); and commencement of the first Tamil Arasu postal service with its own postage stamp. The army began its attack on citizens and arrested the Tamil MPs; placing them again under house arrest for 6 months. In the same year the Language of the Courts Act was enacted making Sinhala as the only language in Court proceedings. Meanwhile the national economy started its decline again with rumours of an armed forces coup d'etat, which was foiled promptly. The outstanding issue of the Stateless citizens question was settled through dialogues with Lal Bahadur Shastri, the Prime Minister of India, resulting in the Sirima-Shastri Pact of 1964. India accepted to take back roughly half of the Stateless up country Tamils, while Sirimavo promised to issue citizenship to the remaining half, resulting in enforced repatriation of Tamils from the estates to neighbouring Tamilnadu.

In December 1964, the SLFP and the leftist coalition lost in the general elections giving way to the UNP under the leadership of Dudley Senanayake, the son of late D.S.Senanayake. This time round he had empowered himself to last the whole hog of government cycle; calling his a national government – having the support of the Tamil Federal Party and the Tamil Congress. The Senanayake-Chelvanayagam Pact was signed along the lines of the Bandaranaike-Chelvanayagam Pact of 1958; in return for the Tamil support for the National government. The UNP government in order to fulfil its pact obligation published the 'District Council Bill' following the enactment of regulations for 'Reasonable use of Tamil'. Opposition to these concessions mounted with the UNP abrogating the Senanayake-Chelvanayagam Pact. With back to square one again, the Federal Party quit the national government in 1969 with the calling of fresh elections; while it's nominee minister in the national government, M.Thiruchelvam stood exposed as a non-achiever. V.Navaratnam-a pro-Eelam MP for Kayts, dissatisfied with the Federal Party resigned and formed the Thamilar Suyaadchi Kazhagam(Tamil Self-rule Party).

While all this was happening; the Tamil émigré population in London began to pile up the necessary foundation for internationalising the Sri Lankan Tamil Issue. The first of such was the sponsoring of the Kodeeswaran Language Rights case to the Privy Council in London; whereby Kodeeswaran a clerical servant and others, refused to study Sinhalese under the Oficial Language Act; and therefore had the salary increment stopped as a punishment. The General Clerical Service Union which Vaikuntha Vasan had help build up; was now infested with Sinhala fascism resulting in the division of the working class. The GCSU refused to take up the Tamil officers' rights. The Tamil clerical servants then made their exit to form the Arasaanga Ezhuthu Vinaygnar Sangam (Government Clerical Servants' Union). Kodeeswaran challenged that the original contract of employment did not stipulate the proficiency in the Sinhala language as a condition. The case which was taken up in 1964 in the Colombo District Court resulted in his favour.

But he was frustrated when the Supreme Court, pleased the government, on its appeal by setting aside the District Court's verdict. The Supreme Court ruled that a government servant has no right to sue the crown; but ignored the constitutional right. So the case was taken to the Privy Council in London. Members of the Arasaanga Eluthu Vinaygnar Sangam raised the finance to send lawyers to London; and the Tamil Action Committee(UK) founded by the Tamil émigré campaigner Sinnappu Maharasingam; and the author Satha Ananthan sponsored the case in London in 1969. Ably pleaded by Queen's Counsel Ranganathan and his team, the Privy Council set aside the Sri Lankan Supreme Court's decision, stating that Kodeeswaran's increment of salary cannot be stopped and that the Sri Lankan Supreme Court should decide on the constitutional issue of whether the Official Language Act was intra vires or ultra vires of Parliament under Section 29 of the Constitution. Focus had now turned on Section 29 of the Soulbury Constitution, which prohibited discrimination against minorities. This verdict, which was a victory for the Tamil clerical servants, also shook the Sinhala politicians. The path therefore had to be paved now for a change of the Constitution in Toto; before the Kodeeswaran case is taken up again.

The Sinhala government had now no other alternative but to remove Section 29 of the Constitution. And Sri Lanka's new ruler Srimavo Bandaranaike (SLFP), who came to power in 1970, decided to turn Sri Lanka into a Republic. As a prelude the Senate-the second Chamber of the Parliament-was abolished in 1971. The Parliament was turned into a Constituent Assembly so as to break the legal continuity of its obligations to the crown; and drafted the new constitution with the active support of the leftist parties. The Republican Constitution was drafted with the abolition of Section 29 in mind; with no minority rights clause enshrined in it. The Tamil Members of

Parliament walked out and boycotted the Assembly. On May 1972 Ceylon officially became a Republic and changed its name to Sri Lanka. As a Republic, appeals to the Privy Council were now made redundant. And the Sinhala leaders won their case without going to the Privy Council again.

In April 1971, Sri Lanka experienced its first leftist socialist insurrection. The Janatha Vimukthi Peramuna(JVP) (People's Liberation Front); a clandestine but popular socialist movement led by Rohana Wijeweera, mobilised the low country Sinhalese belonging to lower castes to rise up against the oppressive upper caste capitalist Sinhala government. 93 police stations were attacked in the South in one day. Stunned Sirimavo Bandaranaike appealed to India for military assistance; and the prompt Indian military assistance saved her government. More than 5,000 Sinhalese youth laid down their lives in the uprising.

Realising the dangers facing from the new Republican Constitution, the Federal Party, Tamil Congress, Ceylon Workers Congress led by S. Thondaman, Eela Thamilar Ottumai Munnani(led by C.Suntharalingam)and the Tamil Maanavar Peravai assembled in Trincomalee in May 1972 to launch the Tamil United Liberation Front (TULF). Back in 1970 the government had already introduced the Standardisation (quotas) of entry to the University, aiming at reducing the Tamils entering on merits. This naturally gave way to Tamil youth forming a resistance front; joining in the political movement with widespread agitations. Meanwhile Jaffna being chosen as the venue for the fourth International Tamil Research Conference, became a focus of the world Tamils, unnerving the government in Colombo. On the penultimate day of the festivities in January 1974, Police unleashed an unprovoked attack on the crowd, creating a pandemonium, resulting in the loss of nine lives. On the youth front; Kaasi Ananthan-the Tamil poet, Sathiaseelan, Maavai Senadhirajah and 45 others were arrested in 1974, following their incessant campaign against the authorities. It was at this time that the young Tamils got inspired by the spontaneously rising fire brand, Sivakumaran, who had taken up to arms against the oppressive Sinhalese military in occupation. Having attempted a Bank raid in Kopay, Sivakumaran was confronted by a Police Inspector; and on the latter's pleading as of being father of daughters to support; merciful Sivakumaran swallowed cyanide instead of shooting down the Inspector. Sivakumaran thus became the first Tamil freedom martyr. Youth leaders like Maha Uthaman, Muthukumaraswamy and Ariaratnam later began to organise Tamil students in the north. Pressurised now by the Tamil youth led by Sathiaseelan, the TULF met in Valvetithurai and declared to strive for a separate Tamil Eelam State and adopted the Rising Sun as the national flag. The TULF followed up with the pledge to establish an independent Tamil State in its 1976 Vaddukoddai resolution. The first political killing took place in Jaffna when Tamil youths fired at the ex-Mayor of Jaffna and the ruling SLFP's agent-Alfred Duraiyappah.

In 1977 the UNP won the elections under the leadership of the wily leader-chieftain of the Sinhalese for the next two decades - Junius Richard Jayawardene. A capitalist to the core with a burning ambition to rule the Island, Jayawardene finally achieved the power that he was seeking for decades. He played the card of communalism (racism) astutely; a treacherous tool invented by the western imperialists to subjugate the masses. Furthermore, he and the Sinhala politicians were enviously incensed at the selection of the TULF leader Appapillai Amirthalingam as the leader of the Opposition, by virtue of having obtained the second largest majority of seats in the House. Amirthalingam's virulent speech in Colombo attacking the Sinhala was the last straw that was now needed to create a riot. Jayawardene made his infamous public statement: 'If you want war we will go to war…' and the third anti-Tamil Riots thus enveloped the Island within a month of his assuming power. Over 100 Tamils lost their lives and more than 50,000 made homeless, including up country plantation workers, who

moved to settle down in the north. In 1978, Jayawardene introduced a new constitution with proportional representation;
changed the Island's name to *Democratic Socialist Republic of
Sri Lanka* and made himself the first Executive President. In
April 1978, a select unit of the Tamil New Tigers (formed as a
fighting unit of the Tamil Maanavar Peravai in 1974) entrapped
and killed the notorious C.I.D Inspector Bastiampillai and his
team. The government reacted by proscribing the Tamil
Tigers;and followed up with the draconian Prevention of
Terrorism Act(PTA)of 1979. An emergency was declared in the
Tamil areas followed by army occupation. Many Tamil youths
were killed indiscriminately. The PTA assumed supremacy over
all other law and courts of law. Under its sweeping powers, the
minister of defence could arrest any person suspected to be acting unlawfully in any way and could be detained incommuni-
cado, without trial for up to 18 months.

Jayawardene's own state sponsored riots afflicted the country
again in 1981 when security forces went on a rampage in Jaffna
city, resulting in the burning of the Jaffna Public Library, con-
taining nearly 100,000 volumes of historical and Tamil cultural
treasure. For the first time, security forces became onlookers
when Sinhala hoodlums attacked Tamils and their homes and
businesses, in many parts of the country. This was now the prelude to the worst to take place-that was the Genocide of 1983.
Meanwhile, following the confident majority achieved from the
referendum he held in December 1982, Jayawardene imposed a
regime of terror in the north; with Tamil militants striking back
killing about 25 security personnel and scaled up their attacks
further. The government introduced the Sixth Amendment thus
proscribing Separatism as illegal.

The Tamil New Tigers (est.1974),had by 1979 moved its spread
across the Palk Strait.Following internal dissensions in 1981;
the Freedom Movement branched in three separate ways:
Liberation Tigers of Tamil Eelam (LTTE) led by Veluppillai

Prabakaran; Peoples' Liberation Organisation of Tamil Eelam (PLOTE) led by Uma Maheswaran and Tamil Eelam Liberation Organisation (TELO) led by Kuttimani. The Liberation Tigers of Tamil Eelam led by Veluppillai Prabakaran, ambushed and blew up an army truck at Thirunelvely, a suburb of Jaffna city on 23rd July 1983. All 13 soldiers died in that first major operation of Tamil Tigers, along with the Tiger unit commander Chella Kili. The Sri Lankan army which had already begun its rampage on Jaffna and Vavuniya in the months preceding, got the fright. The government organised a state funeral for the dead military personnel in Colombo's main cemetery on the following day. Riots erupted following the funeral with armed forces and thugs descending on every Tamil home and business in the capital. Armed with voters lists, several politicians turned into as riot commanders all over the Island. Prominent among them were the Minister of Industries Cyril Mathew and Sunil Ranjan Jayakody an MP. Over 1,000 Tamils were killed and most part of the capital was burning for a few days. 53 Political prisoners, including a highly reputable Social worker Dr. Rajasundaram of Gandhiyam Institution and Kuttimani, the TELO leader, were killed by Sinhalese prisoners. Whole world was shocked at the horrible acts that were committed on innocent Tamils. President Jayawardene, satisfied with the sadistic orgies, eventually called in for law and order. Having enthusiastically pursued a symbiosis of an open-market, export oriented, western capitalist programme, which had only brought immense hardship and repression on his people, Jayawardene found a communal outlet to divert their anger. The Damage was done.

A real exodus of the Tamils of Sri Lanka had now started; adding onto the already exiled population since the 60s. The Tamil Eelam Freedom Movement groups moved its activities into the Tamilnadu state from 1983 onwards. Chennai became a hotbed of the Tamil Eelam freedom movement. Tamil refugees started pouring into the State of Tamilnadu in thousands. Leading politicians in Tamilnadu sympathised with the Tamils from Sri Lanka and extended unprecedented hospitality. Dr. Ira Janarthanan, a campaigner for the Tamil Eelam cause since 1974, and already a host to the first Tamil emigre activist Rajaratnam,acted as the chief co-ordinator. Rajaram and Chengee Ramachandran both Ministers;Chief Minister M.G. Ramachandran and DMK leader M.Karunanithy-all patronised theTamil groups.Two staunch Tamil nationalist leaders P.Nedumaran and V.Gopalaswamy offered intense support for the LTTE. Tamil groups had started setting up training camps in 1982 to raise their own armed battalions and by 1987 there were 32 camps with over 20,000 trained Tamil fighters. The succour and support offered by the people ofsouth India to the Tamil refugees were exemplary.

The second and even more important breeding ground of the Tamil Eelam Freedom Movement was London. The Tamil Eelam Movement had begun in London as far back as 1962, with the Tamil émigré activist Sinnappu Maharasingam establishing the Tamil Action Committee. He had been instrumental in raising the Eelam consciousness among the Tamils of UK ever since. The **London Murasu**, the first Tamil magazine in the West to have been founded by the author Satha Ananthan, in 1970, became the voice and information centre for the Tamil cause for the next two decades. Maharasingam meanwhile enlisted support from some of the British elite; with whose assistance he got the first Minority Rights Group Report published, titled: **The Tamils of Sri Lanka** by Walter Schwarz in 1975. The ice had been broken. But a queer gauntlet of surveillance had already been thrown on the Tamil activists by the British and later by French security, noticeably with the impressive demonstration and burning of the Republican Constitution in front of the Sri Lankan embassy led by Sinnappu Maharasingam, in 1972. The first overseas active freedom unit-the Eelam Revolutionary Organisation (EROS), founded in London in 1975 by E. Ratnasabapathy, a Journalist, also dis turbed the hornest's nest when members of the group established training links with Cuba and Lebanon's PLO. General Union of Eelam Students(GUES) was formed from the EROS to link the Tamil students, which later transcended into as the EPRLF (Eelam People's Revolutionary Front). While all this was happening the Tamil New Tigers had also established its network overseas with London as its vital European centre. Its eventual mentor Anton Stanislaus (Anton Balasingham), a Journalist, had already arrived in London, after a decade of stint as a translator with the British High Commission in Colombo; having worked before that as a sub-editor in the Virakesary, the popular Tamil daily of Sri Lanka. Having had liaisons with a small group called the Tamil Students Congress (South Bank Polytechnic), where Balasingham was studying Psychology; he became the adviser for the Tamil Liberation Organisation (TLO-led by Narayanadas); later moving onto dialoguing with-the General Union of Eelam Students (GUES- led by Maha Uthaman) and finally made contacts with the Tamil New Tigers; and through them established rapport with Veluppillai Prabakaran in 1979.The whole course of events of Tamil freedom movement started taking a galloping momentum from thereon.

It was at this juncture that Krishna Vaikuntha Vasan, senior Judge in the Zambian Judicial system, arrived in London in 1977 and begun his campaign. Concerned with the Tamil Eelam cause he formed the London Committee of Friends of the Tamils (1977) and made contacts with Tamil Eelam and British human rights activists in London. The first researched publication he released: The Way Out for the Tamil Speaking People-INDO-CEYLON FEDERATION, in March 1978, proposed a federal set-up for Tamil Eelam with India and raised the eye brows of many. Next on his agenda was the historic United Nations appearance in October 1978; which was to give an unprecedented boost for the Tamil Eelam cause.

In Tamilnadu, there were now five main groups; LTTE, PLOTE, TELO, EPRLF and EROS; all trained to enter into war with Sri Lankan forces; and enter they did. TELO led by Sabaratnam attacked and captured the Chavakacheri Police Station in 1984 and followed up by mining and destroying a train packed with armed personnel and passengers near Mankulam in 1985. And from then on the war in Sri Lanka escalated with thousands killed on both sides. The Liberation Tigers of Tamil Eelam became the main vanguard in the war- absorbing or eliminating all other groups into oblivion. LTTE had set up an advanced arms procurement network with its own fleet of shipping vessels worldwide and had raised its own Sea Tigers. The liberation war was taken right into the heart of Colombo terrorising the Sinhalese masses and the armed forces. All Party Conferences were hastily called by Sri Lanka and several high-level talks between Sri Lankan, Indian and Tamil groups failed to bring any solution; including the much publicised Thimpu Talks in Bhutan.

In 1987 Jayawardene ordered the Vadamaradchi offensive and killed hundreds of civilians. An economic blockade coupled with carpet bombing forced India to intervene. Rajiv Gandhi ordered the air dropping of food parcels and enforced a treaty with Jayawardene resulting in the Indo-Ceylon Accord and the arrival of the Indian Peace Keeping Force. The Sinhalese psyche was dented with resentment among the armed forces; the new Prime Minister Premadasa became furious; and the wily Jayawardene subtlely played his cards. The tide turned against when twelve LTTE cadres apprehended in a cross channel chase were demanded by the Sri Lankan government to be handed over to them for interrogation. Reluctantly the IPKF agreed to hand over; before which time the LTTE squad committed suicide by swallowing cyanide capsules. The LTTE resented and broke the ceasefire and all hell let loose. The IPKF increased the strength of its forces with the EPRLF as its proxy; but found the staying tough and counter-productive with the Sri Lankan government arming and establishing a queer alliance with the LTTE against the Indian Peace Keeping Force. The new Prime Minister V.P.Singh withdrew the entire Indian Peace Keeping Forces by March 1990 to avert a 'US-in-Vietnam like trap'.

Armed with the huge arsenal of weaponry supplied by the Sri Lankan government itself, the LTTE recommenced their campaign of evicting Sri Lankan security personnel en Toto; while rest of the Tamil militant groups (PLOTE led by Siddharthan;EPDP led by Devananda; TELO and ENDLF) realigned themselves with the Sri Lankan government.Whereas, EROS, led by V.Balakumar merged with the LTTE. In a seesaw of gigantic victories and colossal losses the LTTE and the Sri Lankan government won and lost territories, arsenals and camps with thousands of personnel lost on both sides. Depressingly, the period from 1985 had also seen numerous political, militant and military leaders assassinated or wiped out. Rajiv Gandhi, Premadasa, Amirthalingam, Athulath Mudali and Gamini Dissanayake - all national leaders; Sabaratnam, Padmanabha, Uma Maheswaran, Kittu and Mahathaya (militant leaders); Major General Kobbekaduwa (Army commander) and several dozens more of the elite were killed. But more importantly and sadly over 60,000 sons and daughters of the Sri Lankan soil have so far died and more maimed and disabled as a result of this never ending conflict. The defence budget alone had drained the entire Island's wealth many times over and the whole Island is crippled to the pith.

Peace in Sri Lanka

J.R.Jayawardene, one of the architects for the scale of destruction-the Island had suffered, once said: *Tamils constitute the world's most powerful minority* and so he was right. Additionally to what he pronounced, the Tamil fighters of the LTTE became the most fearsome and powerful guerrilla and resistance force in the world, reminiscing the heroic epics of Sangam literature.In the most daring attack on Katunayake airport and airforce base on July 24th, 2000, the Sri Lankan government lost half the civilian and a third of the military- Aircraft.The national economy slumped with an estimated loss of US$500millions.The tide swiftly turned; with peace as the only alternative. But the massive energies, intelligence and money drained, with the greatest daring sacrifice had not brought a clear victory for theTamils. If the same had been applied;for instance by any other national group, they would have conquered the whole world over many times at ease. What went wrong? The Jaffna Tamil nation, which was the cream and bulk of

the freedom movement had patent deficiencies that were counter-pro
ductive from the very start. Among them was the millennium-old
extreme casteism endemic in the Jaffna society, which had in the
course of its social emancipation emitted venomous caste myopia (a
backlash of revenge by the oppressed on the descendents of the per-
petrators of casteism). This had only intensified the already inherent
trait of internecine rivalry within the Jaffna Tamil society; which was
steeped in a life of a cramped Jaffna peninsula. The Tamil freedom
movement was also deprived of and was in terrible dearth of an
Intelligentsia capable of leading a nation with calmness, perspicacity
and vision. A vision which would have sensed the 'Duttu Gemunu
psyche' deeply rooted in the Sinhalese nation, which in desperation
withstood even the worst; by turning the Tamils against its very own
saviour force- the IPKF; ending in a weird betrayalism, assassination
of Rajiv Gandhi and the resultant mess. The aloofness and caution
with which the Indian Prime Minister Vajpayee is handling the peace
process, letting Norway take the initiative, is proof of the painful
experience India has had. Most importantly Post-September 11th
(2001) had finally daunted on the Western powers-now struggling for
their own self preservation; that the genie of terrorism and guerrilla
warfare that was nurtured and let out from its very own mother centres have now got to be contained and neutralised. Both the Sinhalese
and the Tamils have been losers in the decay that befell the Island
since 1956; with the only winners being the merchants of death -
manufacturing, dealing and brokering the arms procurement; and the
recipient countries of migrants, serving the western capitalistic
wheels of finance, labour and consumer markets. The Sri Lankan
Prime Minister Ranil Wickremasinghe,fully appreciative of the cooperation and fortification offered by Prime Minister Vajpayee is
forging close amity with New Delhi, despite a non-cooperative clamour from President Chandrika Bandaranaike.It is also the spontaneous outcome from his realisation of the devastating predicament
that has descended on the Island. And all parties are now committed
to the peace process. A peace, that will hopefully be a lasting and
deserving gift; for the pearl of the Indian Ocean-Sri Lanka.

Chapter 9
The Legacy of Vaikuntha Vasan: The Rest

Things won are done;
Joy's soul lies in the doing.
- Shakespeare

The legacy of Vaikuntha Vasan was immersed in action; he found joy in the doing. Following his visit to the Peoples' Republic of China and the USSR and taking part in the Vienna Peace Conference; Vaikuntha Vasan decided to widen his horizon. His dismissal from the government service for trade union activities had been made void and the government had re-instated him in service in 1956. But he did not remain in service for long; he made his way to London and qualified himself as a Barrister. In 1965, Vaikuntha Vasan entered into the fray of the General Elections in Ceylon and contested the Kankesanthurai electorate in the north, as a member of the United Left Front. Although he did not succeed, he made an impact on the electorate by endeavouring to signal the message that there was still hope for a united Ceylon through solidarity from the socialist section of the Sinhalese.

Having watched the hope of a united Ceylon gradually sliding into a vain dream, Vaikuntha Vasan emigrated from the Island in 1971, assuming a position in the Zambian Judicial Service. On assuming service Vaikuntha Vasan said: *I have come to Africa, to gain new experience and see a new part of the world that is developing rapidly.* Starting as a senior Resident Magistrate he was promoted year-by-year to become the acting Supreme Court Judge of Zambia. During his assignment in Zambia, Vaikuntha Vasan had brushed shoulders with the high command of Zambia, including President Kenneth Kaunda. He represented Zambia in the Commonwealth Magistrates Conference in Nairobi in August 1973. He had also meetings with Malaysia's Prime Minister-founding father, Tunku Abdul Rahman; and Lord Denning – the innovative and vigorous civil rights lawyer; when he represented Zambia in the fourth Commonwealth Magistrates Conference held in Kuala Lumpur (August 1975). It was while in Zambia that his prodigal artist son Gandeepan(10) presented a portrait of the visiting Indian Prime Minister Indira Gandhi. Having reached the zenith in Zambia; Vaikuntha Vasan saw no reason to stagnate there. He set his eyes on the megalopolis of London, which was not only expanding as the epicentre of global operations, but was also brewing to be a hotbed of nationalist struggles; and so left Zambia in 1976.

Hot on the heels of arriving in his new home in the suburbia of Colliers Wood, in southwest London, in 1977; Vaikuntha Vasan established his Barrister's Chamber in the Strand. He also set up the London Committee of Friends of the Tamils and established contacts with Tamil Eelam activists and British human rights sympathisers. His first research publication: ***The Way Out for the Tamil Speaking People: Indo-Ceylon Federation*** advocated the transformation and broadening of the demand for Eelam as a movement for the merger of Ceylon and India in an Indo-Ceylon Federation. He suggested this in a context of a South Asia group including Pakistan, Bangladesh, Nepal, Burma, Bhutan etc., leading to a South Asian Parliament. This, he said, would be along the lines of the European Parliament. Vaikuntha Vasan, an admirer of Dr. Ananda Coomaraswamy, the international expert on Indian and Ceylonese cultural renaissance, quotes from what he said: *The more I know of Ceylon, the more inseparable from India does it appear and indeed I regret sometimes that Ceylon and India are not at present under one administration. Ceylon is in the truest sense a part of India...in Asia all roads lead to India.* The Report was jointly published by the Eelam Tamils Association(UK) and the Ilankai Thamil Sangam(USA) in March 1978.

In a special reception held in London's Connaught Rooms to the visiting Indian Prime Minister Morarji Desai, in June 1978, Vaikuntha Vasan posed the Federation idea. Morarji Desai rebuffed by saying: *I don't encourage that idea. They(Tamils)should not do this. They are Ceylonese and not Tamilians.* And the idea was shelved. But the relentless Vaikuntha Vasan had planned of a better strategy next and set off to New York in September. What happened later became a historical event in the annals of the United Nations.

In London, Vaikuntha Vasan found bubbling waves of enthusiasm among the Tamils; giving birth to an array of Organisations with regular events of one sort or another. The Organisations in London with substantial activity in the 70s and 80s (with the chief organisers where applicable) were: Tamil Action CommitteeUK(Sinnappu Maharasingam), Eelam Revolutionary Organisation-EROS(E.Ratnasabapathy), Eelam Tamils Association(Maharasingam, N.Ramanathan and others), Tamil United Liberation Front-TULF-UK Branch, Valar Eelam Trust, later merged with the Standing Committee of Tamil Speaking People-SCOT, Dravida Trust, Central British Fund for Tamil Refugees-CBF(K.Kanthasamy and Maharasingam), General Union of Eelam Students-GUES(Thambiah and Maha Uthaman), Silamboli Women's League(Pathma Perinpanayagam and others), Tamil Liberation Organisation-TLO(Narayanadas and others), Tamil Women's League(Rajeswary Balasubramaniam), Tamil Information Centre(V.Varadakumar) and representative offices of TNT/LTTE, PLOTE, TELO and EPRLF. These being the main socio-political organisations of the 1970s and 1980s; not taking into account the non-political entities in the educational, cultural and religious fields. Vaikuntha Vasan entrusted himself with a difficult task of co-ordinating most of the socio-political organisations by forming the Tamil Co-ordinating Committee (TCC), and became the chief co-ordinator. There were occasions when he was seen pleading for and cementing unity, as fissures were menacing to split up organisations.

Vaikuntha Vasan was called to Norway, when a Sri Lankan Tamil girl Java Maria Nainar, under sponsorship by a Norwegian couple was about to be deported. He took up the case forthwith and pleaded with the Norwegian government to let her stay. Java Maria's case hit the headlines in Norway; lead ing to many Norwegians at the helm of power to realise of the happenings in Sri Lanka. Then on Norway's foreign office attention begun to encompass the Sri Lankan Tamil issue.

Having met the Indian Foreign Minister Atal Behari Vajpayee in 1979; the next year Vaikuntha Vasan left for India on his campaign trail. In his stay in New Delhi, Vaikuntha Vasan met the Indian Prime Minister Indira Gandhi and presented a memorandum on the Sri Lankan Tamil issue, which created some furore in the Sri Lankan Press. He also called on the Defence Minister R. Venkataraman, Minister for External Affairs P. V. Narasimha Rao and Sanjay Gandhi; and also addressed the Martin Luther King Memorial meeting in New Delhi. Down in the South, in his whirlwind tour, he met the Tamilnadu Chief Minister M. Karunanithy, Minister Anbazhagan, Pondicherry State Chief Minister Ramachandran and his ministers. He also addressed the Madras University chaired by Sir Muththiah Chettiar. The following year Vaikuntha Vasan was seen immersed in the mammoth Fifth World Tamil Conference held in Madurai under the auspices of M.G.Ramachandran the Chief Minister of Tamilnadu. Vaikuntha Vasan was always on the move.

In 1982, Vaikuntha Vasan had announced to declare a Unilateral Declaration of Independence(UDI) for Tamil Eelam and the formation of an interim government in exile. For this purpose Vaikuntha Vasan chose Chennai as the location. Sensing the consequences, Indira Gandhi ordered Vaikuntha Vasan to be deported to London and he was back again in the headlines of the Press. Interestingly it was days before his deportation that Vaikuntha Vasan had a daylong meeting with the LTTE leader Veluppillai Prabakaran and his deputy, Subramaniam, under the sponsorship of P. Nedumaran, Tamilnadu's chief emissary of the LTTE.

In London, Vaikuntha Vasan had political leaders, campaigners and intelligence agents streaming in for consultations. Among them were: Appapillai Amirthalingam(TULF), Dr. Ira Janarthanan,Siddharthan(PLOTE), Anton Balasingham(LTTE) andRohanGunaratne(SriLanka's powerful National Intelligence Bureau-NIB).Rohan Gunaratne, presently a research scholar on International Terrorism at St.Andrews University, Scotland; has written sensational books on SriLanka, and also on International Terrorism.

Vaikuntha Vasan is a campaigner par excellence was proved when he successfully executed a meeting with Pope, John Paul II in Rome in1983. He gave a detailed memorandum highlighting the Sri Lankan Tamils' plight to the Pope.In his campaign trail, he later contested as an independent candidate in the 1997 general elections for the Mitcham and Morden Parliamentary constituency of London.

In his line of duty, Vaikuntha Vasan had also encouraged the potentials of his prodigal son Gandeepan in portraying leading personalities on canvas as and when the occasion arose. Gandeepan kept close to his father and he had painted the portraits of Indira Gandhi, Kenneth Kaunda, Tamilnadu Chief Minister M. Karunanithi, and Lord Denning-the Master of Rolls- all at a very young age. In London, Gandeepan(23) was chosen among over hundred entries by the City Livery Company, for sittings to draw the portrait of former Prime Minister Harold MacMillan to celebrate his ninetieth birthday in 1985. Gandeepan also drew the portrait of Sabapathi Pillai, the founder of Europe's first Hindu-Shaivite Institution – the Highgate Hill Murugan Temple in London; which portrait beautifies the Temple entrance hall in Highgate. Both portraits had the Royal blessings-the former unveiled by Prince Charles(1985) and the latter viewed by Queen Elizabeth on her Golden Jubilee visit(June 2002) to the Highgate Hill Murugan Temple.

Vaikuntha Vasan still active at 80, was afforded a fitting Eightieth Birthday celebration by the Tamil Community of United Kingdom, on 29th April 2000, at the London Muthumari Amman Temple Hall in Tooting. Many spoke on the great achievements of this legendary figure. But an academic scholar, Prof. Gopan Mahadeva, just spoke of Maheswary Vaikuntha Vasan, his wife for 57 years(2002). *Behind every successful man, there is a woman-is a well-known saying. But Vaikuntha Vasan was blessed with a wife who was not just behind him; but she was always at his side with an ever smiling face, serving, travelling with and inspiring him in every possible manner*. and at times of hardships it was Maheswary who bore all the burdens; She was also in the forefront in the Trade Union marches in Sri Lanka...A whole volume will not suffice to describe the qualities of this ideal wife of Krishna Vaikuntha Vasan.

Epilogue

On the very first sitting of the many sessions with Vaikuntha Vasans we agreed that this book will not be another authorised biography; but instead it will be immensely educative and informative as well. Readers, therefore, would have seen that this treatise is very different, but useful; delving into the relevant fields of Vaikuntha Vasan's action arena.

The climax of Vaikuntha Vasan's life was undoubtedly- the rocking of the United Nations. Therefore, we agreed that the entire gamut of the structure and salients of the United Nations be portrayed. Vaikuntha Vasan relished in the idea that the public will be getting the finest eagle viewed glimpse of the whole of the United Nations encompassed within this book. So we had done that. Acknowledgements are due to the United Nations Association of London, for kindly supplying with the relevant literature needed to make that exercise a success.

The second educative panorama we portrayed was based on Vaikuntha Vasan's three months' visit to China, USSR and Vienna, on a tour de Peace. Peace is the hour of the need worldwide and so the tour had portrayed all that was needed to promote peace. Over and above that, the chapter depicts the true life in the two socialist countries at that time. It is not our intention to advocate communism or capitalism; both being failures. But the chapter exposes the sad state of affairs of the East European populations, now deeply mired with hunger, unemployment, homelessness and corruption; being denied the recourse back to the comparatively higher standard of life they enjoyed earlier on.

Vaikuntha Vasan's campaign trail in the last two decades was to spearhead the Sri Lankan Tamil cause to world at large; which he did so remarkably well. But the world at large has so far not

been given a complete and concise Sri Lankan history on a plat
ter. We have done that in this book. In fact, the history of Sri
Lanka is vividly depicted with forthrightness from as far back
as 4,800 years ago to date. Acknowledgements are due to
Graham Hancock for his marvellous researched publication:
Underworld – Flooded Kingdoms of the Ice Age; which has
enlightened the world with both the greatness of the Indian
civilisation and also of the stages of detachment of the Sri
Lankan Island from its motherland. P. Sathiaseelan, one of the
fountains of the Tamil Freedom movement, and a graduate in
Sri Lankan history, was kind enough to make valuable com-
ments on the chapter on Sri Lanka.

Vaikuntha Vasan's son Gandeepan, a great artist, naturally contributed on the graphic-design sector. He was also a keen and
cheerful participant in our meetings at Colliers Wood. Always
aside her husband was Maheswary Vaikuntha Vasan-a grand
old lady with grace, monumental patience and great understanding. She was his secretary for 57 years long, with no sight
on retirement. And Maheswary had played the most crucial role
in bringing out this publication is not an understatement.
Finally, as always, I have to acknowledge - the inspiration,
typesetting and graphics assistance offered by my wife Gnana
in the creation of this Biography.

So long as there will be a Tamil society, Vaikuntha Vasan's
relentless actions and achievements will be praised. This Book
is dedicated to such a great man-who lived a Life of Purpose.
And is also dedicated to all such great men and women over
there, whom the mega media has failed to recognise and honour. The purpose of this Biography is to inspire all such great
men and women to continue with their great actions - for
History is made by such great men and women.

Index